Ruth Prawer Jhabvala

Heat and Dust

W0316685

Cornelsen

Ruth Prawer Jhabvala **Heat and Dust**

Herausgegeben von:
Reinhold Wandel

Verlagsredaktion:
Neil Porter

Technische Umsetzung:
Ingo Ostermaier

Umschlagillustrationen:
Großes Bild: Merchant Ivory/The Kobal Collection
Kleines Bild: © Wolfgang Kaehler/Corbis

Herausgeber der Cornelsen Senior English Library:
Prof. Dr. Albert-Reiner Glaap

www.cornelsen.de

1. Auflage, 3. Druck 2007/06

Alle Drucke dieser Auflage sind inhaltlich unverändert
und können im Unterricht nebeneinander verwendet werden.

Druck: CS-Druck CornelsenStürtz, Berlin

ISBN 978-3-06-031786-8

Inhalt gedruckt auf säurefreiem Papier aus nachhaltiger Forstwirtschaft.

Contents

Some Introductory Remarks

The novel *Heat and Dust* consists of two parallel plots both of which are set in India, one in the 1920s, the other one about 40 or 50 years later.

The British Administration in India (1920s)

In 1920 India was a British colony, and the British Raj (the Hindi word for 'rule') was based on and maintained by military troops and a civil administration, the Indian Civil Service.

British involvement in the Indian subcontinent had begun in 1600, when merchants set up the East India Company. Over the next 200 years this trading company became so powerful that it controlled large parts of India. In 1858, following the Indian Mutiny, the territories held by the East India Company were officially taken over by the British government and became a crown colony. The Indian Mutiny (called the 'First War of Independence' by many Indians) is often referred to in *Heat and Dust*. The British officers who fought and were killed during this uprising were looked upon as 'heroes of the Empire'.

The chief representative of British rule in India was the Viceroy, who from 1913 onwards was based in New Delhi. India was divided into provinces and districts. The chief administrator of a district was called the district officer or collector. He was the local magistrate who set up courts and tried people for small offences. He collected the taxes (a rather unpopular task which was usually done by his assistant), was responsible for keeping law and order and for giving help and advice to people who came to him. He was supported by a superintendent of police and, sometimes, a medical superintendent. In *Heat and Dust* Mr Crawford is the collector, Douglas his assistant; Mr Saunders is the senior doctor.

The British administrators had their strict duties, but they lived pleasant if not luxurious lives in large, comfortable bungalows, often waited on by a large number of Indian servants. The British usually kept to themselves and had no real relations with the native population.

In the 1920s there were about 600 Indian princes who had more or less semi-autonomous control of their lands – such as the Nawab in *Heat and Dust*. They, however, had to swear loyalty to the British monarch and were politically controlled by the British.

Hippies in India (1970s)

In 1947 India became an independent country, which was mainly due to the protest movement led by Gandhi. Thus the novel's second plot, set in 1970, shows facets and features of postcolonial, independent India. The late 1960s and 1970s were a time when many young people from Europe and the US took the 'hippie trail' to India. (From Europe the backpackers often used the long overland route via Turkey, Iran, Afghanistan and Pakistan, travelling as cheaply as possible and spending the nights in inexpensive, often run-down hostels.) They were motivated by a number of factors: disillusionment with Western materialism, the desire to escape the routine monotony of daily life, the notion of 'finding oneself' and 'communicating with other people'. They hoped to find spiritual insights and inspiration from Hindu 'gurus' (religious teachers). Some of them joined 'ashrams', Hindu religious communities or study centres, and lived there for some time.

This interest in India and Hinduism was intensified when in 1966 first George Harrison and then all the Beatles set off on a musical and spiritual quest in India. They studied Indian music, learned how to play the sitar (and used it in their songs) and took up transcendental meditation. Harrison remained a follower of the Hare Krishna tradition all his life, which is reflected in songs like the 'Hare Krishna Mantra' and 'My Sweet Lord'.

Most of the young people spent only seneral months in India, while a few settled in India or Nepal for years, living on a low budget. Besides the search for spirituality, many young people took drugs such as hash and LSD. Sometimes the emotional and physical strain of being confronted by India with its vast diversity of religions, cultures and languages was too much for the young Westerners; they suffered from culture shock, illness or mental breakdowns. Chid, the young Englishman in *Heat and Dust*, is an example of this experience.

Geographical setting

The story of *Heat and Dust* is set in the fictional towns of Satipur and Khatm, and could be anywhere in India that is unbearably hot and dusty in summer. Other places like Cobabpur, Dhung, and Kafarabad are also fictional.

Naturally, many of the important cities mentioned, such as Bombay, Delhi and Lucknow, are real places and well-known. Indore is a city in the state of Madhya Pradesh, while Amritsar is the capital of the Punjab; Fatehpuri Sikri is world famous for its temples.

Simla, Ooty or Kasauli are the so-called 'hill stations', towns situated in mountainous areas and founded by the British in order to escape from the unbearable heat in the plains. Often only the British women spent the hot season in the cool climate of the hill stations, since the men could not get away from their jobs. Mussoorie and Dharmsala (or Dharamsala) are also mountain towns in the north of India, famous for their pleasant climate and beautiful scenery.

Abbreviations and Annotations

abbr	abbreviation
adj	adjective
cf.	confer; see
derog	derogatory
e.g.	exempli gratia; for example
esp.	especially
etc.	et cetera; and so on
fml	formal
infml	informal
jdm/jdn	jemandem/en
n	noun
p., pp.	page, pages
pl	plural
sb.	somebody
sing	singular
sl	slang
sth.	something
usu.	usually
v	verb

The annotations are arranged chronologically in the stories: the first time a word is used in a story is where you will find it explained.

Shortly after Olivia went away with the Nawab, Beth Crawford returned from Simla. This was in September, 1923. Beth had to go down to Bombay to meet the boat on which her sister Tessie was arriving. Tessie was coming out to spend the cold season with the Crawfords. They had arranged all sorts of visits and expeditions for her, but she stayed mostly in Satipur because of Douglas. They went riding together and played croquet and tennis and she did her best to be good company for him. Not that he had much free time, for he kept himself as busy as ever in the district. He worked like a Trojan and never ceased to be calm and controlled, so that he was very much esteemed both by his colleagues and by the Indians. He was upright and just. Tessie stayed through that cold season, and through the next one as well, and then she sailed for home. A year later Douglas had his home leave and they met again in England. By the time his divorce came through, they were ready to get married. She went out to join him in India and, like her sister Beth, she led a full and happy life there. In course of time she became my grandmother – but of course by then everyone was back in England.

I don't remember Douglas at all – he died when I was three – but I remember Grandmother Tessie and Great-Aunt Beth very well. They were cheerful women with a sensible and modern outlook on life: but nevertheless, so my parents told me, for years they could not be induced to talk about Olivia. They shied away from her memory as from something dark and terrible. My parents' generation did not share these feelings – on the contrary, they were eager to learn all they could about Grandfather's first wife who had eloped with an Indian prince. But it was not until they were old and widowed that the two ladies began at last to speak about the forbidden topic.

1 **Nawab**: the title of a (Muslim) nobleman or governor in India 2 **Simla**: summer capital of India situated on the edge of the Himalayas 6 **Satipur**: fictional Indian town 9 **Trojan** (old-fashioned): person who works very hard **cease**: stop
10 **esteemed**: respected and admired 22 **induce sb.**: persuade sb. 23 **shy away from sth. (shied – shied)**: avoid sth. because you are nervous or frightened of it
26 **elope**: run away with sb.

By that time they had also met Harry again. They had kept up with him by means of Xmas cards, and it was only after Douglas' death that Harry came to call on them. They spoke about Olivia. Harry also told them about Olivia's sister, Marcia, whom he had met shortly after his return from India. He had continued to see her over the years till she had died (drunk herself to death, he said). She left him all Olivia's letters and he showed them to the old ladies. That was how I first came to see these letters which I have now brought with me to India.

Fortunately, during my first few months here, I kept a journal so I have some record of my early impressions. If I were to try and recollect them now, I might not be able to do so. They are no longer the same because I myself am no longer the same. India always changes people, and I have been no exception. But this is not my story, it is Olivia's as far as I can follow it.

These are the first entries in my journal:

2 February. Arrival in Bombay today. Not what I had imagined at all. Of course I had always thought of arrival by ship, had forgotten how different it would be by plane. All those memoirs and letters I've read, all those prints I've seen. I really must forget about them. Everything is different now. I must get some sleep.

Woke up in the middle of the night. Groped for my watch which I had put on top of my suitcase under the bed: it wasn't there. Oh no! Not already! A voice from the next bed: 'Here it is, my dear, and just be more careful in future please.' Half an hour after midnight. I've slept about four hours. Of course I'm still on English time so it would be now about seven in the evening. I'm wide awake and sit up in bed. I'm in the women's dormitory of the S.M. (Society of Missionaries) hostel. There are seven string beds, four one side three the other. They're all occupied and everyone appears to be asleep. But outside the city is still awake and restless. There is even music somewhere. The street lamps light up the curtainless windows of the dormitory from outside, filling the room

21 **grope for sth.**: try and find sth. that you cannot see by feeling with your hands
27 **dormitory**: room in which several people sleep

with a ghostly reflection in which the sleepers on their beds look like washed-up bodies.

But my neighbour – the guardian of my watch – is awake and wanting to talk:

'You've probably just arrived, that's why you're so careless. Never mind, you'll learn soon enough, everyone does. … You have to be very careful with your food in the beginning: boiled water only, and whatever you do, no food from these street stalls. Afterwards you get immune. I can eat anything now if I want to. Not that I'd want to – I hate their food, I wouldn't touch it for anything. You can eat here in the S.M., that's quite all right. Miss Tietz looks after the kitchen herself and they make nice boiled stews, sometimes a roast, and custard. I always stay here when I come to Bombay. I've known Miss Tietz for twenty years. She's Swiss, she came out with the Christian Sisterhood but these last ten years she's been looking after the S.M. They're lucky to have her.'

It may be due to the ghostly light that she looks like a ghost; and she's wearing a white night-gown that encases her from head to foot. She has tied her hair in one drooping plait. She is paper-white, vaporous – yes, a ghost. She tells me she has been in India for thirty years, and if God wants her to die here, that is what she will do. On the other hand, if He wants to bring her home first, she will do that. It is His will, and for thirty years she has lived only in His will. When she says that, her voice is not a bit ghost-like but strong and ringing as one who has been steadfast in her duty.

'We have our own little chapel out in Kafarabad. It's a growing town – because of the textile mills – but not growing in virtue, that I can tell you. Thirty years ago I might have said there is hope: but today – none. Wherever you look, it's the same story. More wages means more selfishness, more country liquor, more cinema. The women used to wear

2 **washed-up bodies**: dead bodies that have been brought to the shore by the waves 3 **guardian**: person who protects sb./sth. 8 **street stall**: table or small shop (e.g. in a market) with an open front from which people sell things
12 **stew**: Eintopf **custard** (esp. BE): Vanillesoße 17 **encase sb./sth.**: cover sb./sth. completely 18 **plait** [plæt]: Zopf **vaporous** ['veɪpərəs]: dunstig
24 **steadfast**: very loyal

plain simple cotton dhotis but now they all want to be shiny from the outside. We won't speak about the inside. But why expect anything from these poor people when our own are going the way they are. You've seen that place opposite? Just take a look.'

I go to the window and look down into the street. It's bright as day down there, not only with the white street lights but each stall and barrow is lit up with a flare of naphtha. There are crowds of people; some are sleeping – it's so warm that all they have to do is stretch out, no bedding necessary. There are a number of crippled children (one boy propelling himself on his legless rump) and probably by day they beg but now they are off duty and seem to be lighthearted, even gay. People are buying from the hawkers and standing there eating, while others are looking in the gutters to find what has been thrown away.

She directs me to the other window. From here I get a view of A.'s Hotel. I had been warned about that place before I came. I had been told that, however bleak and dreary I might find the S.M. Hostel, on no account should I book myself into A.'s.

'Can you see?' she called from her bed.

I saw. Here too it was absolutely bright, with street and shop lamps. The sidewalk outside A.'s was crowded – not with Indians but with Europeans. They looked a derelict lot.

She said 'Eight, nine of them to a room, and some of them don't even have the money for that, they just sleep on the street. They beg from each other and steal from each other. Some of them are very young, mere children – there may be hope for them, God willing they'll go home again before it's too late. But others there are, women and men, they've been here for years and every year they get worse. You see the state they're in. They're all sick, some of them dying. Who are they, where do they come from? One day I saw a terrible sight. He can't have been more than thirty, perhaps a German or Scandinavian – he was very

1 **dhoti**: piece of simple clothing worn on the lower part of the body by some Indian men 7 **barrow**: Karren **naphtha** ['næfθə]: inflammable oil that produces a bright light 10 **rump**: Rumpf 11 **gay** (old-fashioned): cheerful, happy 12 **hawker**: person who carries goods from place to place and tries to sell them 13 **gutter**: Gosse, Rinnstein 16 **bleak**: cold and depressing **dreary**: sad, cheerless 21 **derelict lot**: heruntergekommener Haufen

fair and tall. His clothes were in tatters and you could see his white skin through them. He had long hair, all tangled and matted; there was a monkey sitting by him and the monkey was delousing him. Yes the monkey was taking the lice out of the man's hair. I looked in that man's face – in his eyes – and I tell you I saw a soul in hell. Oh but I've seen some terrible sights in India. I've lived through a Hindu-Muslim riot, and a smallpox epidemic, and several famines, and I think I may rightly say I've seen everything that you can see on this earth. And through it all I've learned this one thing: you can't live in India without Christ Jesus. If He's not with you every single moment of the day and night and you praying to Him with all your might and main – if that's not there, then you become like that poor young man with the monkey taking lice out of his hair. Because you see, dear, nothing human means anything here. Not a thing,' she said, with the contempt of any Hindu or Buddhist for all this world might have to offer.

She was sitting up in her bed. For all she was so thin and white, she did look tough, toughened-up. A ghost with backbone. I looked down again at the figures sprawled under the white street lights outside A.'s Hotel. It seemed to me that she was right: they did look like souls in hell.

16 February. Satipur. I have been very lucky and have already found a room here. I like it very much. It is large, airy, and empty. There is a window at which I sit and look down into the bazaar. My room is on top of a cloth-shop and I have to climb up a flight of dark stairs to get to it. It has been sub-let to me by a government officer called Inder Lal who lives with his wife and mother and three children in some poky rooms crammed at the back of a yard leading from the shop. The shop belongs to someone else and so does the yard. Everything is divided and

1 **in tatters**: old and torn 2 **tangled**: zerzaust **matted**: verfilzt 3 **delouse sb./sth.**: take lice (= Läuse) out of the hair/fur of sb./sth. 7 **smallpox epidemic**: Pockenepidemie **famine**: Hungersnot 11 **with all your might and main**: with all your strength 14 **contempt**: Geringschätzung, Verachtung 17 **toughened-up**: made tough and strong 18 **sprawled**: ausgestreckt 24 **flight**: series of steps 25 **sub-let sth.**: etwas untervermieten 26 **poky**: very small and not very comfortable 27 **crammed**: full of things or people

sub-divided, and I'm one of the sub-divisions. But I feel very spacious and private up here; except that I share the bathroom facilities down in the yard, and the little sweeper girl who is attached to them.

I think my landlord, Inder Lal, is disappointed with the way I live in my room. He keeps looking round for furniture but there isn't any. I sit on the floor and at night I spread my sleeping-bag out on it. The only piece of furniture I have so far acquired is a very tiny desk the height of a foot-stool on which I have laid out my papers (this journal, my Hindi grammar and vocabulary, Olivia's letters). It is the sort of desk at which the shopkeepers do their accounts. Inder Lal looks at my bare walls. Probably he was hoping for pictures and photographs – but I feel no need for anything like that when all I have to do is look out of the window at the bazaar below. I certainly wouldn't want to be distracted from that scene. Hence no curtains either.

Inder Lal is far too polite to voice his disappointment. All he said was 'It is not very comfortable for you,' and quickly lowered his eyes as if afraid of embarrassing me. He did the same when I first arrived with my luggage. I had not hired a coolie but had hoisted my trunk and bedding on to my shoulders and carried them up myself. Then too – after an involuntary cry of shock – he had lowered his eyes as if afraid of embarrassing me.

It would have been easier for him if I had been like Olivia. She was everything I'm not. The first thing she did on moving into their house (the Assistant Collector's) was smother it in rugs, pictures, flowers. She wrote to Marcia: 'We're beginning to look slightly civilised.' And again, later: 'Mrs. Crawford (Collector's wife – the *Burra Memsahib*) came to

1 **spacious**: having a lot of room 3 **sweeper girl**: girl that has to sweep the toilet and to keep it clean 13 **distract sb.**: jdn. ablenken 18 **coolie**: unskilled native worker **hoist sth.**: lift sth. **trunk**: large box or suitcase 20 **involuntary**: unabsichtlich 24 **Assistant Collector**: In the Indian Civil Service the Collector was responsible for collecting taxes. He had a powerful role, because collecting taxes showed that the British controlled India in a very direct way; he was therefore unpopular. The 'assistant collector' is the assistant of the collector, usu. a younger man (new to India) starting his career at this position. **smother sth.**: cover sth. **rug**: Teppich 26 **Burra memsahib** (Hindi): 'great madam' (term of respect used by Indians for European married women)

inspect me today in my nest. I don't think she thinks much of me *or* the nest but she's ever so tactful! She told me she knows how difficult the first year always is and that if there is any little thing she could possibly do to ease things for me, well I must just consider her to be always *there*. I said thank you (demurely). Actually, her being there is the only difficult thing – otherwise everything is just *too perfect*! If only I could have told her that.'

I have already seen the house in which Douglas and Olivia lived. In fact, there has been a very lucky coincidence – it turns out that the office where Inder Lal works is right in what used to be the British residential area (known as the Civil Lines). Inder Lal's own department, Disposal and Supplies, is in what was the Collector's house (Mr. Crawford's, in 1923). Douglas and Olivia's bungalow now houses the Water Board, the municipal Health Department, and a sub-post office. Both these houses have, like everything else, been divided and sub-divided into many parts to fulfil many functions. Only the Medical Superintendent's house has been kept intact and is supposed to be a travellers' resthouse.

20 February. This morning I dropped in on the two ladies of the Inder Lal family – his wife, Ritu, and his mother. I don't know whether I caught them at a moment of unusual confusion or whether this is the way they always live but the place was certainly very untidy. Of course the rooms are poky and the children still at the messy stage. Ritu swiftly cleared some clothes and toys off a bench. I would have preferred to sit on the floor as they did, but I realised that now I had to submit to all the social rules they thought fit to apply to my case. The mother-in-law, in a practised hiss aside, gave an order to the daughter-in-law which I guessed to be for my refreshment. Ritu darted out of the room as if glad to be released, leaving me and the mother-in-law to make what we could of each other. We smiled, I tried out my Hindi (with scant success

5 **demure**: wohlerzogen 11 **residential area**: area where people live 14 **water board**: administration of the waterworks **municipal**: städtisch
17 **superintendent**: Leiter/in 23 **swift**: fast 27 **hiss aside**: zur Seite zischen
28 **dart**: move or go quickly 30 **scant**: little

– I must work harder at it!), we made hopeful gestures, and got nowhere. All the time she was studying me. She has a shrewd, appraising glance – and I can imagine how she must have gone around looking over girls as possible wives for her son before finally deciding on Ritu. Quite instinctively, she was adding up *my* points as well, and alas I could guess what her sum came to.

I have already got used to being appraised in this way in India. Everyone does it everywhere – in the streets, on buses and trains: they are quite open about it, women as well as men, nor do they make any attempt to conceal their amusement if that is what one happens to arouse in them. I suppose we must look strange to them, and what must also be strange is the way we are living among them – no longer apart, but eating their food and often wearing Indian clothes because they are cooler and cheaper.

Getting myself a set of Indian clothes was one of the first things I did after settling down in Satipur. I went to the cloth-stall downstairs and then next door where there is a little tailor sitting on a piece of sacking with his machine. He measured me right there and then in his open shop in full view of the street, but with such care to keep his distance that his measures were too approximate for any kind of fitting. As a result my clothes are very loose indeed but they serve their purpose and I'm glad to have them. I now wear a pair of baggy trousers tied with a string at the waist such as the Punjabi peasant women wear, and their kind of knee-length shirt. I also have a pair of Indian sandals which I can shuffle off and leave on thresholds like everyone else. (They are men's sandals because the women's sizes don't fit me). Although I'm now dressed like an Indian woman, the children are still running after me; but I don't mind too much as I'm sure they will soon get used to me.

There is one word that is often called after me: *hijra*. Unfortunately I know what it means. I knew before I came to India, from a letter of

2 **shrewd, appraising glance**: scharfsinniger, abwägender Blick 5 **alas**: expression of fear or sorrow 10 **conceal sth.**: hide sth. 17 **sacking** (n): cloth, canvas 23 **Punjabi**: people who live in north-western India 30 **hijra** (Hindi): eunuch, transvestite

Olivia's. *She* had learned it from the Nawab who had told her that Mrs. Crawford looked like a *hijra* (Great-Aunt Beth was, like me, tall and flat-chested). Of course Olivia also didn't know what it meant, and when she asked, the Nawab shouted with laughter. But instead of explaining he told her 'I will show you,' and then he clapped his hands and gave an order and after some time a troupe of *hijras* was brought and the Nawab made them sing and dance for Olivia in their traditional style.

I have also seen them sing and dance. It was when I was walking back with Inder Lal from seeing his office. We were quite near home when I heard a noise of drums from a sidestreet. Inder Lal said it was nothing worth looking at – 'a very common thing,' he said – but I was curious so he reluctantly accompanied me. We went through a succession of alleys winding off from each other and then we entered an arched doorway and went down a passage which opened up into an inner courtyard. Here there was the troupe of *hijras* – eunuchs – doing their turn. One played a drum, others sang and clapped their hands and made some dancing motions. There was a cluster of spectators enjoying the performance. The *hijras* were built like men with big hands and flat chests and long jaws, but they were dressed as women in saris and tinsel jewellery. The way they danced was also in parody of a woman's gestures, and I suppose that was what amused people so much. But I thought their faces were sad, and even when they smirked and made suggestive gestures to what I guessed to be suggestive words (everyone laughed and Inder Lal wanted me to come away), all the time their expression remained the worried workaday one of men who are wondering how much they are going to be paid for the job.

24 February. Today being Sunday, Inder Lal kindly offered to take me to Khatm to show me the Nawab's palace. I felt bad about taking him away from his family on his one day off, but neither he nor they seemed to think anything of it. I wonder his wife does not get tired of being shut up in her two small rooms all day and every day, with her mother-in-law

6 **troupe**: group, band 12 **reluctant**: zögerlich 12–13 **succession**: series
13 **wind** [waɪnd] (v): have a curving and twisting shape 17 **cluster**: small group
19 **jaw**: Kiefer **tinsel**: glitter 22 **smirk**: grinsen

and three small children. I never see her go out anywhere except sometimes – accompanied by her mother-in-law – to buy vegetables in the bazaar.

I have not yet travelled on a bus in India that has not been packed to bursting-point, with people inside and luggage on top; and they are always so old that they shake up every bone in the human body and every screw in their own. If the buses are always the same, so is the landscape through which they travel. Once a town is left behind, there is nothing till the next one except flat land, broiling sky, distances and dust. Especially dust: the sides of the bus are open with only bars across them so that the hot winds blow in freely, bearing desert sands to choke up ears and nostrils and set one's teeth on edge with grit.

The town of Khatm turned out to be a wretched little place. Of course Satipur isn't all that grand either, but it does give a sense of having been allowed to grow according to its own needs. But Khatm just huddles in the shadow of the Nawab's palace. It seems to have been built only to serve the Palace, and now that there is no one left in there, doesn't know what to do with itself. The streets are dense, run-down, and dirty. There are many, many beggars.

Protected by high pearl-grey walls, the Palace is set in spacious grounds with many tall trees. There are fountains and water channels, garden pavilions, and a little private mosque with a golden dome. Inder Lal and I sat down under a tree while the watchman went off to find the keys. I asked Inder Lal about the Nawab's family but he doesn't know much more than I do. After the Nawab's death in 1953, his nephew Karim, who was still an infant at the time, inherited the Palace. But he never lived there. In fact, he lives in London where I met him just before coming out here (I will write about that later). The family are still negotiating with the Government of India for a sale, but so far, over all

4–5 **packed to bursting-point**: very full 7 **screw**: Schraube 9 **broil**: be very hot 10 **bar**: Gitterstange 11–12 **choke up sth.**: etwas verstopfen 12 **set sb.'s teeth on edge**: (of a sound or taste) make sb. feel physically uncomfortable **grit**: mixture of dust and sand 13 **wretched**: miserable 16 **huddle**: gather closely together 18 **dense**: containing a lot of people 22 **dome**: Kuppel

these years, no price has been agreed upon. There are no other bidders: who would want a place like this nowadays – and in Khatm?

Inder Lal was not keen to discuss the Nawab. Yes, he had heard about him and his dissolute bad life; also vague rumours about the old scandal. But who cares about that now? All those people are dead, and even if any of them should still be left alive somewhere, there is no one to be interested in their doings. Inder Lal was much more interested to tell me about his own troubles which are many. When the man arrived with the keys, we walked around the Palace and now I saw all the halls and rooms and galleries I have thought about so much and tried to imagine to myself. But the place is empty now, it is just a marble shell. The furnishing has been sold off in European auction rooms, and all that is left, here and there like shipwrecks floating in the marble halls, are some broken Victorian sofas and the old cloth fans – pull-*punkahs* – hanging dustily from the ceiling.

Inder Lal walked close behind me and told me about the goings-on in his office. There is a lot of intrigue and jealousy. Inder Lal would like not to get involved – all he asks is to be allowed to carry out his duties – but this is impossible, people will not let him alone, one is forced to take sides. As a matter of fact, there is a lot of jealousy and intrigue against him too as the head of his department is favourably disposed towards him. This is very galling to Inder Lal's fellow officers who would do anything – such is their nature – to pull him down.

We stood on an upper gallery overlooking the main drawing room. The watchman explained that here the ladies of the household used to sit concealed behind curtains to peer down at the social entertainment below. One curtain was still left hanging there – a rich brocade, stiff with dust and age. I touched it to admire the material, but it was like touching something dead and mouldering. Inder Lal – who was just telling me about the head of his department whose mind is unfortunately

1 **bidder**: person that offers to pay an amount of money to buy sth. 4 **dissolute**: ausschweifend 14 **fan**: Fächer **pull-punkah**: large swinging fan that is fixed to the ceiling and pulled by a servant during hot weather 21–22 **be favourably disposed to(wards) sb.**: jdm. wohlgesonnen sein 22 **galling**: annoying **fellow officer**: Amtskollege 27 **brocade**: thick, heavy fabric 29 **moulder** (v): rot, decay

being poisoned by interested parties – also touched the curtain. He commented: 'Ah, where has it all gone?' – a sentiment which was at once echoed by the watchman. But then both of them decided that I had seen enough. When we got out into the garden again – as green and shady as the Palace was white and cool – the watchman began rather urgently to speak to Inder Lal. I asked about the Nawab's private mosque, but Inder Lal informed me that this would not be interesting and that instead the watchman would now show me the little Hindu shrine he had fixed up for his own worship.

I don't know what this place had been originally – perhaps a store-room? It was really no more than a hole in the wall and one had to stoop to get through the opening. Several other people crowded in with us. The watchman switched on an electric light bulb and revealed the shrine. The principal god – he was in his monkey aspect, as Hanuman – was kept in a glass case; there were two other gods with him, each in a separate glass case. All were made of plaster-of-paris and dressed in bits of silk and pearl necklaces. The watchman looked at me expectantly so of course I had to say how nice it was and also donate five rupees. I was anxious to get out as it was stifling in there with no ventilation and all these people crowded in. Inder Lal was making his obeisances to the three smiling gods. He had his eyes shut and his lips moved devoutly. I was given some bits of rock sugar and a few flower petals which I did not of course like to throw away so that I was still clutching them on the bus back to Satipur. When I thought Inder Lal was not looking, I respectfully tipped them out the side of the bus, but they have left the palm of my hand sticky and with a lingering smell of sweetness and decay that is still there as I write.

8 **shrine**: Schrein 9 **worship**: act of showing respect to a god, esp. by saying prayers, singing, etc. 11 **stoop**: sich bücken 13 **reveal sth.**: show sth. that before could not be seen 14 **Hanuman**: monkey god, worshipped by Hindus
16 **plaster-of-paris**: gebrannter Stuckgips 18 **donate sth.**: give sth. (e.g. money, food) for charity **rupee**: Indian currency 19 **stifling** ['staɪflɪŋ]: hot and airless 20 **obeisance**: gesture to show respect 21 **devout**: andächtig 22 **petal**: Blütenblatt 23 **clutch sb./sth.**: hold onto sb./sth. tightly 26 **lingering**: lasting, remaining 27 **decay**: Verfall

1923

Olivia first met the Nawab at a dinner party he gave in his palace at Khatm. She had by that time been in Satipur for several months and was already beginning to get bored. Usually the only people she and Douglas saw were the Crawfords (the Collector and his wife), the Saunders (the Medical Superintendent), and Major and Mrs. Minnies. That was in the evenings and on Sundays. The rest of the time Olivia was alone in her big house with all the doors and windows shut to keep out the heat and dust. She read, and played the piano, but the days were long, very long. Douglas was of course extremely busy with his work in the district.

The day of the Nawab's dinner party, Douglas and Olivia drove over to Khatm with the Crawfords in the latter's car. The Saunders had also been invited but could not go because of Mrs. Saunders' ill health. It was a drive of about 15 miles, and Douglas and the Crawfords, who had all of them been entertained by the Nawab before, were being stoic about the uncomfortable journey as well as about the entertainment that lay ahead of them. But Olivia was excited. She was in a travelling costume – a cream linen suit – and her evening dress and satin shoes and jewel case were packed in her overnight bag. She was glad to think that soon she would be wearing them and people would see her.

Like many Indian rulers, the Nawab was fond of entertaining Europeans. He was at a disadvantage in not having much to entertain them with, for his state had neither interesting ruins nor was it hunting country. All it had was dry soil and impoverished villages. But his palace, which had been built in the 1820s, was rather grand. Olivia's eyes lit up as she was led into the dining room and saw beneath the chandeliers the long, long table laid with a Sèvres dinner service, silver, crystal, flowers, candelabras, pomegranates, pineapples, and little golden bowls of crystallised fruits. She felt she had, at last in India, come to the right place.

24 **impoverished**: verarmt 26 **chandelier**: Kronleuchter 27 **Sèvres**: French town famous for its porcelain 28 **candelabra**: Armleuchter, Tafelleuchter **pomegranate**: Granatapfel

Only the guests were not right. Besides the party from Satipur, there was another English couple, Major and Mrs. Minnies, who lived near Khatm; and one plump, balding Englishman called Harry something who was a house guest of the Nawab's. Major and Mrs. Minnies were very much like the Crawfords. Major Minnies was the political agent appointed to advise the Nawab and the rulers of some adjacent small states on matters of policy. He had been in India for over twenty years and knew all there was to know about it; so did his wife. And of course so did the Crawfords. Their experience went back several generations, for they were all members of families who had served in one or other of the Indian services since before the Mutiny. Olivia had met other such old India hands and was already very much bored by them and their interminable anecdotes about things that had happened in Kabul or Multan. She kept asking herself how it was possible to lead such exciting lives – administering whole provinces, fighting border battles, advising rulers – and at the same time to remain so dull. She looked around the table – at Mrs. Crawford and Mrs. Minnies in their dowdy frocks more suitable to the English watering places to which they would one day retire than to this royal dining table; Major Minnies and Mr. Crawford, puffy and florid, with voices that droned on and on confident of being listened to though everything they were saying was, Olivia thought, as boring as themselves. Only Douglas was different. She stole a look at him: yes, *he* was right. As always, he was sitting up very straight; his nose was straight, so was his high forehead; his evening jacket fitted impeccably. He was noble and fair.

Olivia was not the only one admiring Douglas. The Nawab's house guest, the Englishman called Harry someone who was sitting next to her, whispered to her: 'I *like* your husband.' 'Oh do you?' Olivia said. 'So

3 **plump**: overweight **balding**: losing your hair 6 **appointed**: bestimmt, ernannt **adjacent** [ə'dʒeɪsnt]: neighbouring 11 **Mutiny**: the Indian rebellion against the British of 1857 (**mutiny**: Meuterei) 13 **interminable**: lasting a long time and therefore boring 15 **administer sth.**: govern sth., manage the affairs of sth (esp. a state) 17 **dowdy**: unattractive, unfashionable **frock**: (old-fashioned) dress 18 **watering places**: seaside resorts or spa towns 20 **puffy**: (an)geschwollen **florid**: (of a person's face) red 25 **impeccable**: faultless, perfect

do I.' Harry picked up his napkin from his knees and giggled into it. He whispered from behind it: 'Quite a change from our *other* friends,' and his eyes swept over the Crawfords and the Minnies and when they came back to Olivia he rolled them in distress. She knew it was disloyal, but she could hardly help smiling in reply. It was nice to have someone feel the same way as herself; she hadn't so far met anyone in India who did. Not even, she sometimes could not help feeling, her Douglas. She looked at him again where he sat listening to Major Minnies with attention and genuine respect.

The Nawab, at the head of his table, also appeared to be listening to his guest with attention and respect. In fact, he was leaning forward in his eagerness not to miss a word. When Major Minnies' story turned amusing – he was telling them about a devilish clever Hindu moneylender in Patna who had attempted to outwit the Major many, many years ago when the latter was still green behind the ears – the Nawab, to mark his appreciation of the Major's humour, threw himself far back in his chair and rapped the table; he only interrupted his laughter in order to invite his other guests to join him in it. But Olivia felt he was putting it on: she was almost sure of it. She saw that, while he seemed to be entirely engrossed in listening to the Major, he was really very alert to what was going on around his table. Always the first to see an empty glass or plate, he would give a swift order: usually with a glance, though sometimes he rapped out, sotto-voce, some Urdu word of command. At the same time he took in each one of his guests, and it seemed to Olivia that he had already come to his own conclusions with regard to them all. She would have loved to know what those conclusions were but suspected that he would take good care to dissemble them. Unless of course she got to know him really well. His eyes often rested on her, and she let him study her while pretending not to notice. She liked it – as she had liked the way he had looked at her when she had first come in. His eyes had

4 **distress**: feeling of worry and unhappiness 16 **appreciation**: Anerkennung, Wertschätzung 17 **rap sth.**: hit sth. with your hand 18 **put it on**: pretend
20 **engrossed**: so interested in sth. that you give it all your attention **alert**: aufmerksam 23 **sotto-voce** [ˌsɒtəʊ ˈvəʊtʃi] (Italian): halblaut, gedämpft **Urdu**: language (similar to Hindi) spoken by Muslims in Pakistan and India
27 **dissemble sth.**: hide sth.

lit up – he checked himself immediately, but she had seen it and realised that here at last was one person in India to be interested in her the way she was used to.

After this party, Olivia felt better about being alone in the house all day. She knew the Nawab would come and call on her, and every day she dressed herself in one of her cool, pastel muslins and waited. Douglas always got up at crack of dawn – very quietly, for fear of waking her – to ride out on inspection before the sun got too hot. After that he went to the court-house and to his office and was usually too rushed to come home again till late in the evening and then always with files (how hard they worked their district officers!). By the time Olivia woke up, the servants had cleaned the house and let down all the blinds and shutters. The entire day was her own. In London she had loved having hours and hours to herself – she had always thought of herself as a very introspective person. But here she was beginning to dread these lonely days locked up with the servants who padded around on naked feet and respectfully waited for her to want something.

The Nawab came four days after the party. She was playing Chopin and when she heard his car she went on playing with redoubled dash. The servant announced him and when he entered she turned on her piano stool and opened her wide eyes wider: 'Why Nawab Sahib, what a lovely surprise.' She got up to greet him, holding out both hands to him in welcome.

He had come with a whole party (she was to learn later that he was usually attended). It included the Englishman, Harry, and then there were various young men from the Palace. They all made themselves at home in Olivia's drawing room, draping themselves in graceful attitudes over her sofas and rugs. Harry declared himself charmed with her room

6 **muslin**: type of fine cotton fabric 10 **file**: Akte, Ordner 12 **blind** (n) Markise, Verdunklung **shutter**: Fensterladen 14 **introspective**: inward-looking; tending to think a lot about yourself and your feelings 16 **pad**: walk steadily and softly 18 **Frédéric Chopin** (1810–1849): French-Polish composer, who wrote mostly piano music 19 **redoubled dash**: doppelte Geschwindigkeit 21 **sahib**: term of respect for a man 27 **drape yourself**: (here) sit or place yourself loosely but elegantly

– he loved her black and white prints, her Japanese screen, her yellow chairs and lampshades. He flopped into an armchair and, panting like a man in exhaustion, pretended he had crossed a desert and had at last reached an oasis. The Nawab also seemed to enjoy being there. They stayed all day.

It passed in a flash. Afterwards Olivia could not recall what they had talked about – Harry seemed to have done most of the talking and she and the Nawab had laughed at the amusing things he said. The other young men, who knew little English, could not take much part in the conversation but they made themselves useful mixing drinks the way the Nawab liked them. He had made up a special concoction, consisting of gin, vodka, and cherry brandy, which he also invited Olivia to taste (it was too strong for her). He had brought his own vodka because he said people never seemed to have it. He had taken possession of one of the sofas and sat right in the middle of it with both arms extended along the back and his long legs stretched out as far as they would go. He looked very much at ease, and entirely the master of the scene – which of course he was. He invited Olivia not only to drink his concoction but also to make herself quite comfortable on the sofa facing his and to enjoy Harry's humour and whatever other entertainment the day might bring forth.

That evening Douglas found Olivia not as usual half in tears with boredom and fatigue but so excited that for a moment he feared she had a fever. He put his hand on her brow: he had seen a lot of Indian fevers. She laughed at him. When she told him about her visitor, he had his doubts – but seeing how gay she was, how glad, he decided it was all right. She was lonely, and it was decent of the Nawab to have called on her.

A few days later another invitation from the Palace arrived for them both. There was a charming note with it, to say that if they would do him the honour and happiness of accepting, the Nawab would of course

1 **screen**: Wandschirm 2 **flop**: sich plumpsen lassen 3 **exhaustion**: feeling of being worn out and tired 6 **in a flash**: very fast 11 **concoction**: mixed drink 17 **at ease**: relaxed, easy-going 23 **fatigue**: great tiredness 27 **decent**: well-mannered

be sending a car for them. Douglas was puzzled: he said the Crawfords would as usual be taking them in their car. 'Oh good heavens, darling,' Olivia said impatiently, 'you don't think *they've* been asked, do you.' Douglas stared in amazement: whenever he was amazed like that, his eyes popped a bit and he stuttered.

Later, when it was clear that the Crawfords had really not been invited, he was uneasy. He said he didn't think he and Olivia could accept. But she insisted, she was determined She said she wasn't having such a grand time here – 'believe *me*, darling' – that she felt inclined to miss the chance of a little entertainment when it came her way. Douglas bit his lip; he knew she was right but it was a dilemma for him. He couldn't see how they could possibly go, he tried to explain to her; but she wouldn't hear him. They argued about it to and fro. She even woke up early in the morning so as to go on arguing. She walked with him to the front of the house where his syce stood holding his horse. 'Oh Douglas, *please*,' she said, looking up at him in the saddle. He could not answer her because he could not promise her anything. Yet he longed to do so. He watched her turn back into the house; she was in her kimono and looked frail and unhappy. 'I'm a brute,' he thought to himself all day. But also that day he sent a note to the Nawab, regretfully declining the invitation.

* * * *

28 February. One of the old British bungalows in the Civil Lines has not been converted, like the others, into municipal offices but into a travellers' rest-house. An ancient watchman has been hired to keep it clean and open it up for travellers. But he is not keen on these duties and prefers to be left to himself to spend his time in his own way. When a traveller presents himself, the watchman asks for the official permit; if

5 **pop**: move quickly and suddenly outwards 13 **to and fro**: hin und her
15 **syce** [saɪs]: Indian servant who looks after horses 19 **frail**: weak, poor in health
brute: Unmensch, brutaler Kerl 20 **decline sth.**: refuse sth. 23 **convert sth.**: change sth. 27 **permit** (n): official statement that gives permission for sth.

this is not produced, he considers his responsibilities at an end and shuffles back into the hut where he lives rather snugly.

Yesterday I came across an odd trio outside the travellers' bungalow. The watchman having refused to open the doors, they had had to spread themselves and their belongings out on the verandah. They were a young man and his girl, both English, and another youth who was also English – he spoke in a flat Midlands accent – but wouldn't admit to it. He said he had laid aside all personal characteristics. He had also laid aside his clothes and was dressed in nothing but an orange robe like an Indian ascetic; he had shaved his head completely, leaving only the Hindu tuft on top. But although he had renounced the world, he was as disgruntled as the other two about the watchman who wouldn't let them in. The girl was particularly indignant – not only about this watchman but about all the other people all over India. She said they were all dirty and dishonest. She had a very pretty, open, English face but when she said that it became mean and clenched, and I realised that the longer she stayed in India the more her face would become like that.

'Why did you come?' I asked her.

'To find peace.' She laughed grimly: 'But all I found was dysentery.'

Her young man said 'That's all anyone ever finds here.'

Then they both launched into a recital of their misadventures. They had been robbed of their watches in a house of devotion in Amritsar; cheated by a man they had met on the train to Kashmir who had promised them a cheap houseboat and had disappeared with their advance; also in Kashmir the girl had developed dysentery which was probably amoebic; they got cheated again in Delhi where a tout, promising them a very favourable rate of exchange for their money, disappeared with it by the back door of the coffee house where they had met him; in Fatehpur Sikri the girl had been molested by a party of Sikh youths; the young man's pocket was picked on the train to Goa; in Goa he had got

2 **snug**: small and comfortable 10 **ascetic**: Asket 11 **tuft**: Haarbüschel **renounce sth.**: etwas abschwören 12 **disgruntled** (adj): annoyed 13 **indignant**: angry 16 **clenched**: verkrampft 19 **dysentery**: Durchfall 21 **recital** [rɪ'saɪtl]: spoken description of a series of events 22 **devotion**: Frömmigkeit 25 **advance** (n): Vorauszahlung, Anzahlung 26 **tout** [taʊt]: (here) person who deal with money in an inofficial manner 29 **molest sb.**: (here) touch sb. sexually

into a fight with a mad Dane armed with a razor, and had also been laid up with something that may have been jaundice (there was an epidemic); the girl had contracted ringworm.

At this point the watchman came out of his hut where he seemed to have been cooking himself a tasty meal. He said it was forbidden to stay on the verandah. The young Englishman gave a menacing laugh and said 'Try and get us out then.' Though somewhat worn with sickness, he was a big young man, so the watchman stood sunk in thought. After a while he said it would cost them five rupees to camp on the verandah, including drinking water from the well. The Englishman pointed to the locked doors and said 'Open'. The watchman retreated to get on with his cooking and perhaps ponder his next step.

The young man told me that he and his girl friend had become very interested in the Hindu religion after attending a lecture by a visiting swami in London. It had been on Universal Love. The swami, in a soft caressing voice very suitable to the subject, told them that Universal Love was an ocean of sweetness that lapped around all humanity and enfolded them in tides of honey. He had melting eyes and a smile of joy. The atmosphere was also very beautiful, with jasmine, incense, and banana leaves; the swami's discourse was accompanied by two of his disciples one of whom softly played a flute while the other, even more softly, beat two tiny cymbals together. All the disciples were ranged around the swami on the platform. They were mostly Europeans and wore saffron robes and had very pure expressions on their faces as if cleansed of all sin and desire. Afterwards they had sung hymns in Hindi which were also about the flowing ocean of love. The young man and his girl had come away from this meeting with such exalted feelings that they could not speak for a long time; but when they could, they agreed

1 **razor**: Rasiermesser 2 **jaundice** ['dʒɔːndɪs]: Gelbsucht 3 **ringworm**: infection of the skin caused by fungus (= Pilz) 6 **menacing** (adj): threatening 11 **retreat**: go back, move back 12 **ponder sth.**: think about sth. 15 **swami**: Hindu religious teacher 16 **caressing**: moving and loving 17 **lap around sth.**: etwas umschließen/umgeben 18 **tide**: Flut 19 **incense**: Weihrauch 20 **discourse**: speech, talk 22 **cymbal**: Becken **range**: sit in an arranged way 24 **saffron**: safranfarben 25 **cleanse sb./sth. of sth.**: make sb./sth. clean from sth. **hymn** [hɪm]: religious song 27 **exalted**: full of joy and happiness

that, in order to find the spiritual enrichment they desired, they must set off for India without delay.

The ascetic said he too had come for a spiritual purpose. In his case, the original attraction had come through the Hindu scriptures, and when he arrived in India, he had not been disappointed. It seemed to him that the spirit of these scriptures was still manifest in the great temples of the South. For months he had lived there, like an Indian pilgrim, purifying himself and often so rapt in contemplation that the world around him had faded away completely. He too developed dysentery and ringworm but was not bothered by them because of living on such a high plane; similarly, he was not bothered by the disappearance of his few possessions from the temple compound where he lived. He found a guru to give him initiation and to strip him of all personal characteristics and the rest of his possessions including his name. He was given a new Indian name, Chidananda (his two companions called him Chid). From now on he was to have nothing except his beads and the begging bowl in which he had to collect his daily food from charitable people. In practice, however, he found this did not work too well, and he had often to write home for money to be sent by telegraphic order. On the instruction of his guru, he had set off on a pilgrimage right across India with the holy cave of Amarnath as his ultimate goal. He had already been wandering for many months. His chief affliction was people running after and jeering at him; the children were especially troublesome and often threw stones and other missiles. He found it impossible to live simply under trees as instructed by his guru but had to seek shelter at night in cheap hotel rooms where he had to bargain quite hard in order to be quoted a reasonable price.

6 **the scriptures**: the holy books of a religion **manifest** (adj; fml): visible, noticeable 8 **purify sb./sth.**: jdn./etwas läutern/reinigen **rapt**: giving your whole mind **contemplation**: intensives Nachdenken 9 **fade away**: disappear or die gradually 12 **compound**: area belonging to a particular building 13 **guru**: spiritual guide **initiation**: religiöse Einführung 17 **beads** (pl): Gebetsperlen 21 **Amarnath:** cave in Kashmir which contains an ice figure that is considered holy 23 **affliction**: Kummer **jeer at sb.**: call sb. names, make fun of sb. 24 **missile**: Wurfgeschoss

The watchman returned, holding up three fingers to signify that the charge for staying on the verandah had now been reduced to three rupees. The Englishman again pointed at the locked doors. But negotiations had begun, and now it was not long before the watchman fetched his keys. Actually, it turned out to be more pleasant on the verandah. It was musty and dark inside the bungalow; the place smelled dead. In fact, we did find a dead squirrel on the floor of what must have been a dining room (there was still a sideboard with mirrors and a portrait of George V inset). It was a gloomy, brooding house and could never have been anything else. From the back verandah there was a view of the Christian graveyard: and I saw rearing above all the other graves the marble angel that the Saunders had ordered from Italy as a monument over their baby's grave. Suddenly it struck me that this dark house must have been the one in which Dr. Saunders, the Medical Superintendent, had lived. I had not realised that Mrs. Saunders had been able to look out at her baby's grave right from her own back verandah.

Of course at that time the marble angel had been new and intact – shining white with wings outspread and holding a marble baby in its arms. Now it is a headless, wingless torso with a baby that has lost its nose and one foot. All the graves are in very bad condition – weed-choked, and stripped of whatever marble and railings could be removed. It is strange how, once graves are broken and overgrown in this way, then the people in them are truly dead. The Indian Christian graves at the front of the cemetery, which are still kept up by relatives, seem by contrast strangely alive, contemporary.

6 **musty**: muffig 8 **sideboard**: Anrichte 9 **inset** (adj): eingelassen **gloomy**: dark and depressing **brooding**: sad and mysterious 11 **rear**: aufragen
21–22 **weed-choked**: von Unkraut überwuchert 22 **railing**: small metal fence

1923

Olivia had always been strongly affected by graveyards. In England too she had liked to wander through them, reading the inscriptions and even sitting on a grave stone under a weeping willow and letting her imagination roam. The graveyard at Satipur was especially evocative. Although Satipur had always been a small station for the British, quite a few of them had died there over the years; and bodies were also brought in from other districts with no Christian cemetery of their own. Most of the graves were of infants and children, but there were also several dating from the Mutiny when a gallant band of British officers had died defending their women and children. The newest grave was that of the Saunders' baby, and the Italian angel was the newest, brightest monument.

The first time Olivia saw this baby's grave, it had a powerful effect on her. That evening Douglas found her lying face down across their bed; she had not allowed the servants to come in and open the shutters, so the room was all closed in and stifling and Olivia herself bathed in tears and perspiration.

'Oh Douglas', she said, 'what if we have a baby?'; and then she cried: 'Yes and what if it should die!'

It took him a long time to soothe her. He had to forget his files for that one evening and devote himself entirely to her. He said everything he could think of. He told her that nowadays babies did not die so often. He himself had been born in India, and his mother had had two other children here and all of them had thrived. It was true, in the old days a lot of children did die – his great-grandmother had lost five of her nine children; but that had been a long time ago. 'What about Mrs. Saunders' baby?'

'That could have happened anywhere, darling. She had – complications – or something –'

4 **weeping willow**: Trauerweide 5 **roam**: wander **evocative**: erinnerungsträchtig 10 **gallant**: tapfer 17 **stifling**: hot and airless 18 **perspiration**: sweat 21 **soothe sb.**: calm sb. 22 **devote yourself to sb./sth.**: sich jdm./etwas widmen 25 **thrive**: do well and be healthy

'I'll have complications. I'll die. The baby and I both.' When he tried to protest, she insisted: 'No, if we stay here, we'll die. I know it. You'll see.' When she saw the expression on his face, she made an effort to pull herself together. She even tried to smile. She put up her hand to stroke his cheek: 'But you want to stay.'

He said eagerly 'It's just that it's all new to you. It's easy for the rest of us because we all know what to expect. But you don't, my poor darling.' He kissed her as she lay there resting against his chest. 'You know, I'd been talking about this very thing with Beth Crawford. (No, darling, you mustn't think that way about Beth, she's a good sort). She knew before you came how difficult it would be for you. And you know what she said *after* you came? She said she was sure that someone as sensitive and intelligent as you are – you see she does appreciate you, darling – that you would surely be ... all right here. That you – well, this is what *she* said – that you'd come to feel about India the way we all do. Olivia? Are you asleep, darling?'

She wasn't really but she liked lying against his chest, both of them shrouded within their white mosquito net. The moon had risen from behind the peach tree and its light came pouring in through the open windows. When Douglas thought she was asleep, he hugged her tighter and could hardly stifle a small cry – as if it were too much happiness for him to have her there in his arms, flooded and shining in Indian moonlight.

Next day Olivia went to visit Mrs. Saunders. She took flowers, fruit, and a heart full of tender pity for her. But although Olivia's feelings towards Mrs. Saunders had changed, Mrs. Saunders herself had not. She was still the same unattractive woman lying in bed in a bleak, gloomy house. Olivia, always susceptible to atmosphere, had to struggle against a feeling of distaste. She did so hate a slovenly house, and Mrs. Saunders' house was very slovenly; so were her servants. No one bothered to put Olivia's pretty flowers in a vase – perhaps there was no vase? There

10 **sort** (infml): person 18 **shroud sb./sth.**: cover or hide sb./sth. 21 **stifle sth.**: etwas unterdrücken 27 **bleak**: miserable, unpleasant 28 **susceptible**: empfänglich 29 **slovenly** ['slʌvnli]: untidy, messy

wasn't much of anything, just a few pieces of ugly furniture and even those were dusty.

Olivia sat by Mrs. Saunders' bedside and listened to her tell about her illness which was something to do with her womb. It had never got right after the baby's death – this was the only mention of the baby's death, for the rest it was all about the bad after-effects on Mrs. Saunders' health. While she talked, Olivia had the unworthy thought that the Saunders really were not – were not – well, no one ever said this outright but they were just not the sort of people usually found in the Indian services. Olivia was by no means a snob but she *was* aesthetic and the details Mrs. Saunders gave about her illness were not; also Mrs. Saunders' accent – how could one help noticing with her droning on and on? – was not that of a too highly educated person ...

I'm base, *base*, Olivia scolded herself – but at that moment she had a shock for Mrs. Saunders gave a loud shout: turning round, Olivia saw that one of the slovenly servants had come in, wearing slovenly shoes. It was these latter that had upset his mistress – and of course it was a mark of disrespect for a servant to enter a room with shoes on, Douglas would never have allowed it to happen in their house. But Olivia was amazed and frightened by the strength of Mrs. Saunders' reaction. She had sat up in bed and was shouting like a madwoman. She called the servant a dirty name too. The servant was frightened and ran away. Mrs. Saunders sank her head down on her pillow in exhaustion, but her outburst was not over yet. She seemed to feel the need to express or perhaps justify herself; she may have been ashamed of the dirty word that had escaped her. She said that these servants really were devils and that they could drive anyone crazy; that it was not stupidity on their part – on the contrary, they were clever enough when it suited their purposes – but it was all done deliberately to torment their masters. She gave examples of their thieving, drinking, and other bad habits. She told Olivia about the filth in which they lived inside their quarters – but of course what could one expect, everything was like that, everywhere the same – the whole

4 **womb**: Gebärmutter 12 **drone on**: talk at length about sth. in a boring voice 14 **base**: bad, mean **scold sb.**: jdm. schelten 29 **deliberate**: intentional; done on purpose **torment sb.**: jdn. quälen 30 **thieving** (n): act of stealing 31 **filth**: dirt, rubbish

town, the lanes and bazaars, and had Olivia ever looked inside one of their heathen temples? Mrs. Saunders groaned and she covered her face with her hands and then Olivia saw that tears came oozing through her fingers and her chest inside her nightgown was heaving with heavy sobs. She brought out 'I've asked him – over and over – I've said: Willie, let's *go*.'

Olivia stroked Mrs. Saunders' pillow and now her tears were flowing too, in pity for someone so unhappy.

What a relief, after that, to be with bright, brisk Beth Crawford! She had come to invite Olivia to accompany her to Khatm, to pay a call on the Nawab's mother. Olivia loved visiting the Palace again, even though this time they were ushered straight into the ladies' quarters. These were also very elegant, though more in Indian style with floor-level divans covered in rich textures, and little mirrors in enamelled frames. Three good European chairs had been arranged in the centre: these were for Mrs. Crawford and Olivia, and for the Begum herself. There were some other, mostly elderly ladies and they reclined on the divans spread on the floor. The younger ladies floated around in diaphanous silks and served sherbet and other refreshments from a succession of trays carried in by servants.

Olivia could do nothing but sit perched up on her chair. Conversation was impossible since she did not know a word of the language. The Begum did try to speak a few words of English to her – only at once to laugh at herself for pronouncing them so badly. She was a woman in her fifties who would have been handsome except for a large wart on her cheek. She was chain-smoking cigarettes out of a holder. She had a very relaxed manner and made no secret of the fact that sitting on a chair was

2 **heathen**: heidnisch **groan**: stöhnen **3 ooze** [u:z]: flow slowly 4 **sob** (n): Schluchzer 9 **relief**: Erleichterung **brisk**: practical and confident 10 **pay a call on sb.**: visit sb. 12 **usher sb. into sth.**: jdn. in etwas hineinbegleiten 13 **divan**: Diwan 14 **texture**: Gewebe **enamelled**: emailliert 16 **Begum** ['beɪgəm]: title of an Indian Muslim lady of high rank 17 **recline**: lie down and stretch out 18 **float**: move in an easy, graceful way **diaphanous** [daɪ'æfənəs]: durchscheinend 19 **sherbet**: cool fizzy or iced fruit drink 21 **perch**: sit like a bird 25 **wart**: Warze

uncomfortable for her. She kept shifting around, tucking now one leg under her and now the other. Olivia, who loved lounging, would also have preferred to recline on the floor but probably it would not have been etiquette.

Mrs. Crawford sat bolt upright on her chair, her stockinged knees pressed together and her hands in white gloves folded on the handbag in her lap. She was the dominant figure in the room on whom the success of the visit depended. And she did not shirk her responsibility. She spoke Urdu (the language of the Palace) if not well at any rate with confidence, and was prepared to give the ladies whatever conversation she thought they might like to hear. Evidently she had come prepared with a variety of topics, for she passed easily from one to the other as interest appeared to wax or wane. The Begum on her chair and the ladies on the floor appeared pleased, and often they laughed out loud and clapped their hands together. Everyone played their part well – the Palace ladies as well as Mrs. Crawford – and gave evidence of having frequently played it before. Only Olivia, the newcomer, could not participate; in any case, her attention was quite a lot on the door, wondering whether the Nawab was going to come in and join them. But this did not happen. At exactly the right moment Mrs. Crawford got up whereat the ladies exclaimed to the right pitch of disappointment; after some protests, they gracefully gave in and accompanied their guests the correct distance to the door. Olivia whispered 'Do we have to call on the Nawab too?' but Mrs. Crawford said firmly 'That will not be necessary at all.' She strode ahead with the step of one who has fulfilled a duty well, while Olivia, trailing behind her, looked right and left – probably to admire the Nawab's flowers which were indeed splendid.

After this visit, they drove to the Minnies' house just outside Khatm. Mrs. Minnies was sitting at her easel but jumped up at once to greet

1–2 **tuck a leg under her**: ein Bein unterschlagen 2 **lounge**: sit in a lazy way
5 **bolt upright**: kerzengerade **stockinged**: covered by stockings (= Strümpfe)
8 **shirk sth.**: sich vor etwas drücken 13 **wax or wane**: grow stronger or weaker
20 **whereat** (old use): at which 21 **pitch**: Tonhöhe 22 **give in**: sich fügen, nachgeben 26 **trail behind sb.**: walk behind sb., follow sb. 29 **easel** ['i:zl]: Staffelei

them. She dismissed her model – a patient old peasant – and taking off her artist's smock, tossed it aside with a girlish gesture. Mrs. Crawford too, now that she was with her friend, became rather girlish. She comically rolled her eyes up as she recounted where they had been, and Mrs. Minnies said 'Oh you *are* good, Beth.' 'It wasn't too bad,' Mrs. Crawford said brightly, and she turned to Olivia: 'was it?' not wanting her to feel left out.

But Olivia did feel left out – just as much as she had done in the Palace. Mrs. Crawford and Mrs. Minnies were such good friends. They had both been in India for years and were cheerful and undaunted. Probably they would have preferred to put their feet up and have a cosy chat of their own, but instead they devoted their attention to Olivia. They had a lot of good advice to give her – about putting up her *khas tatti* screens for the hot weather, and how to instruct the *ayah* to wash her crêpe-de-chine blouses (which must under no circumstances be given to the *dhobi*). Olivia tried to be interested but she wasn't, and at the first possible opportunity she asked a question of her own. She said 'Isn't the Nawab married?'

This brought a pause. The two other ladies did not exchange glances and Olivia felt they didn't have to because of being united in thought. Finally Mrs. Crawford replied 'Yes he is but his wife doesn't live with him.' She spoke in a direct way, like one who doesn't want to gloss over anything. 'She is not very well,' she added, 'mentally.'

'Oh Beth guess what!' Mrs. Minnies suddenly exclaimed. 'I've heard from Simla, and Honeysuckle Cottage is available again this year, isn't that splendid ... Does Olivia have Simla plans?'

Mrs. Crawford answered for her: 'Douglas has been asking about our arrangements.'

'Well there's always a corner for her at Honeysuckle Cottage. Especially now that it looks as if Arthur may not be able –'

1 **dismiss sb.**: send sb. away 2 **smock**: (Maler)kittel **toss sth. aside**: throw sth. off in a careless way 10 **undaunted**: still enthusiastic in spite of difficulties
13–14 **khas tatti screen**: screen (= Wandschirm) or mat (= Matte) which is kept wet to cool the air 14 **ayah**: native female servant 15 **crêpe-de-chine**: thin silk
16 **dhobi**: washerman 22 **gloss over sth.**: etwas vertuschen/beschönigen

'Mary – no! '

'We're still hoping but I'm afraid it doesn't look too good. But *I'm* certainly going,' she said. 'I've never really done the view from Prospect Hill and this year I simply must. Whatever the Nawab might be up to.'

'The Nawab?' Olivia asked.

After a pause Mrs. Minnies told Mrs. Crawford 'There have been new developments. It now looks as if he really is involved.'

'With the dacoits? Mary, how *awful*. And just at this time.'

'Can't be helped,' said Mrs. Minnies with practised cheerfulness. 'I suppose we're used to it by now. Or ought to be. Three years ago it was the same. Our Friend always seems to choose this particular time, when Arthur's leave is due. It's become quite a habit with him.'

Olivia asked 'What happened three years ago?'

After a silence Mrs. Crawford replied – not willingly but as if conceding Olivia's right to know: 'That's when there was all the fuss over his marriage breaking up.' She sighed; obviously the subject was distasteful to her. 'Mary really knows more about it than I do.'

'Not that much more,' Mrs. Minnies said. 'It's always difficult to know what *is* going on ...' She too was reluctant to say more, but she too seemed to feel that Olivia had a right to information: 'Poor Arthur got rather involved, along with Colonel Morris who is his opposite number at Cabobpur, the state belonging to Sandy's family. Sandy is the Nawab's wife. She's always called that though her real name is Zahira.'

'If it hadn't been for Arthur and Colonel Morris,' Mrs. Crawford said, 'the situation could have turned into something quite ugly. The Cabobpurs were absolutely furious with the Nawab.'

'But why?' Olivia asked. 'I mean – it couldn't have been his fault – if she was – mentally not well. . .'

After another pause Mrs. Crawford said 'As Mary says, it's always difficult to know *what's* going on. And there was also some question of

8 **dacoit** [də'kɔɪt] (Indian English): armed robber, bandit 12 **due**: expected to happen or take place 14–15 **concede sth.**: etwas zugestehen 15 **fuss**: unnecessary excitement and activity 19 **reluctant**: zögerlich

return of dowry – it was all very tiresome. … Olivia,' she said, 'you *will* be joining us in Simla, won't you?'

Olivia fidgeted a little; she played with the slim bracelet on her slim arm. 'Douglas and I've been talking about it.'

'Yes and he does so hope you will.' Mrs. Crawford looked at Olivia, and there was something about her look – straight and steady – that was reminiscent of Douglas.

'I wouldn't like to leave him,' Olivia said. 'Four *months* – it seems an eternity.' She added shyly, again fidgeting with her bracelet, 'We haven't been – together so very long.' She was going to say 'married' but 'together' sounded better.

The other two exchanged glances; they laughed. Mrs. Crawford said 'We must seem like a couple of tough old hens to you.'

'Yes but even this tough old hen,' Mrs. Minnies said, 'will feel rather seedy if Arthur can't make it –'

'Why can't he?' Olivia asked.

'We need you, Olivia,' Mrs. Crawford said. 'Life would be deadly in Simla without you.'

'Oh rather,' Mrs. Minnies took up the joke. 'Who will follow *us* down the Mall? Who will call on *us* at Honeysuckle Cottage?'

'Only the other tough old hens.'

They went off into school-prefect laughter. Olivia understood that actually they would be happier without her, doing matronly things and being comfortable with each other. But they were speaking for *her* sake.

She asked 'Is Mrs. Saunders going?'

'No. Joan doesn't come to Simla. Though it would do her so much good to get out of that *house* … You too, Olivia,' Mrs. Crawford added and gave her another Douglas kind of look.

'But why can't Major Minnies go? If it's his leave –' They seemed not to have heard. They began to discuss their Simla plans again – principally,

1 **dowry**: Mitgift **tiresome**: making you feel annoyed 3 **fidget**: herumzappeln 7 **reminiscent of sb.**: reminding you of sb./sth. 14–15 **feel seedy**: sich unwohl fühlen 22 **school prefect**: older student at school with authority over younger students 23 **matronly**: matronenhaft 24 **for sb.'s sake**: jdm. zuliebe 30 **principally**: mainly, mostly

which servants to take with them and which to leave behind to look after the poor old Sahibs who had to stay and sweat it out in the plains.

Olivia got the information she wanted from another source. One dull morning – she was even giving up the piano – she had a visitor. It was Harry, and he came in one of the Nawab's cars driven by the Nawab's chauffeur. He said he simply had to come and refresh himself at the Oasis (which is what he called her house). And she, seeing him, felt that *he* – though plump and unattractive – was an oasis for her. He spent the day, and in the course of it talked of many things that she wanted to hear about.

About the Nawab's wife he said: 'Poor Sandy. Poor thing. It was too much for her. *He* was too much for her.'

'Who?' Olivia poured him another drink – they were having a sweet sherry.

Harry shot her a look, then lowered his eyes: 'He's a very strong person. Very manly and strong. When he wants something, nothing must stand in his way. Never; ever. He's been the Nawab since he was fifteen (his father died suddenly of a stroke). So he's always ruled, you see; always been the ruler.' He sighed, in a mixture of admiration and pain.

'The Cabobpur family didn't want her to marry him,' he said. 'They're much bigger royals of course – he doesn't really count in those circles: not much of a title, and by their standards he isn't even rich.'

'He seems rich,' Olivia said.

'I met him in London first,' Harry said. 'They were all at Claridges – he'd brought everyone with him – everyone he liked, that is, and all the servants he needed like Shafi who mixes his drinks. And the Cabobpurs were there too – on the floor below: they'd brought all their people – but after a week they went away to Paris because of Sandy getting too fond. As if one could run away from someone like him. The next day he was in Paris too. He said to me "You come along, Harry." He liked me, you see.'

'And you went?'

2 **plains**: Ebene 18 **stroke**: Schlaganfall 25 **Claridges**: a traditional grand hotel in London

Harry shut his eyes: 'I told you: one does not say no to such a person. ... By the way, Olivia, Mrs. Rivers ... I may call you Olivia? I do feel we're friends. One feels that with people, don't you think? If they're one's type? ... Olivia, he wants to give a party.'

There was a pause. Olivia poured more sherry. 'He most particularly wants you to come. Of course there'll be a car.'

'Douglas is dreadfully busy.'

'He wants you both to come. He wants it most awfully ... It's strange, isn't it: you'd think someone like him would have a million friends. But he doesn't.'

'*You*'re there.'

Olivia had already asked Douglas what Harry's position was in the Nawab's palace. Was it anything official, like secretary? Douglas had not been very forthcoming, and when she had insisted, he had said 'There are always hangers-on around those people.'

Harry became confidential – he seemed glad to be able to speak freely to someone: 'I do want to do everything I can to make him – happier. Goodness knows I try. Not only because I like him very much but because he's been fantastically kind to me. You can have no idea of his generosity, Olivia. He wants his friends to have everything. Everything he can give them. It's his nature. If you don't want to take, he's terribly hurt. But how can one take so much? It makes one feel ... After all, I'm here because I *like* him, not for any other reason. But all he knows is giving. Giving things.' His face and voice were full of pain.

'But that means he likes you.'

'Who knows? With him you can't tell. One moment you think: Yes he cares – but next moment you might as well be some ... object. I've been with him three years now. Three years, can you imagine, at Khatm. I haven't even seen the Taj Mahal. We keep getting ready to go to oh all sorts of places – but at the last moment something always comes up. Usually it's the Begum who doesn't want us to go ... Do you know, sometimes I feel that the only person he really cares for on this earth is

7 **dreadfully**: very 14 **forthcoming**: willing to give information about sth.
16 **confidential**: showing that what you are saying is private or secret
20 **generosity**: Großzügigkeit

the Begum. He hates to be away from her. Naturally, his mother … I haven't seen *my* mother for three years. I'm worried about her because she hasn't been keeping too well. She's on her own, you see, in a little flat in South Ken. Of course she wants me to come home. But whenever I mention it, all he does is send her some marvellous present. Once she wrote to him – she thanked him but said "The best present you could send me would be my Harry home again." He was really touched.'

'But he didn't let you go?'

Harry gave her a sideways look. He was silent – he even bit in his lips. Then he said 'I hope I didn't give you the impression that I'm complaining.' His tone was prim, offended.

It was by now late in the afternoon and the day was turning stale. She had given him luncheon of which he had eaten very little; apparently he suffered with his digestion. Now it was very hot and close in the room, but it was still too early to open the blinds. The sherry was warm and sticky and so was the smell of the flowers with which she had filled her vases (Olivia could not live without flowers). Now she wanted Harry to go. She wanted the day to be over and that it would be night with a cool breeze blowing and Douglas sitting at his desk rather stern and serious over his interminable files.

Douglas spoke Hindustani very fluently. He had to because he was constantly dealing with Indians and was responsible for settling a great variety of local problems. All his work was of course carried out in his office, or in the courts, or out on site, so Olivia never came in contact with it; but from time to time – usually on festive occasions – some of the local rich men would come to pay their respects. They would sit on the verandah with their offerings to the Sahib which were baskets of fruits and trays of sweetmeats and pistachio nuts. The rich men all

4 **South Ken = South Kensington**: area in central London 5 **marvellous**: amazing, wonderful 11 **prim**: steif 13 **luncheon** (fml): Mittagessen
14 **digestion** [daɪˈdʒestʃən]: Verdauung 19 **stern**: strict, serious 20 **interminable**: never ending 21 **Hindustani** (old-fashioned; now: **Hindi**): main language spoken in (the north of) India 26 **pay your respects**: make a formal visit 28 **sweetmeat**: Leckereien, Süßigkeiten

seemed to look the same: they were all fat, and wore spotless loose white muslin clothes, and shone with oil and jewellery. When Douglas went out to greet them, they simpered and joined their hands together and seemed so overcome with the honour he was doing them that they could barely stammer out their appreciation of it.

Olivia listened to them talking out there. Douglas' voice, firm and manly, rose above the rest. When he spoke, the others confined themselves to murmurs of agreement. He must have made some jokes because every now and again they all laughed in polite unison. Sometimes he seemed to speak rather more sternly, and then the murmurs became very low and submissive till he made another joke whereupon they dissolved in relieved laughter. It was almost as if Douglas were playing a musical instrument of which he had entirely mastered the stops. He also knew the exact moment to start on the finale and there was a shuffle of feet and a last rather louder chorus of gratitude which came out so sincere, so overflowing from a fullness of heart, that some of the voices broke with emotion.

When Douglas came back in, he was smiling. He always seemed to enjoy these encounters. He said 'What a pack of rogues they are,' and shook his head in benign amusement.

Olivia was sitting at her sampler. She had lately taken up embroidery and was making, as her first effort, a floral tapestry cover for a footstool. Douglas sat down in his chair opposite her; he said 'As if I didn't know what they're all up to.'

'What?' Olivia asked.

'Their usual tricks. They're full of them. They think they're frightfully cunning but really they're like children.' He smiled and knocked out his pipe on the English brass fender.

3 **simper**: einfältig lächeln 5 **stammer out sth.**: etwas stammeln/stottern
7–8 **confine yourself to sth.**: sich auf etwas beschränken 8 **murmur**: whisper, talk softly 9 **in unison**: together 11 **submissive**: unterwürfig **whereupon** (old-fashioned) woraufhin 12 **dissolve**: sich auflösen 14 **stop**: Griffloch
19 **rogue**: Schurke 20 **benign** [bɪ'naɪn]: gütig 21 **sampler**. Stickmustertuch **embroidery**: Stickerei 22 **floral**: with flowers **tapestry**: Wandteppich **footstool**: Schemel 27 **cunning**: clever at deceiving others 28 **brass**: Messing **fender**: Kamingitter

'Oh really, darling,' Olivia protested.

'Sorry, darling.' He thought she meant the pipe – he had made a mess with the ash, he was a recent and inexpert smoker – but she didn't. She said 'They look like very grown-up men to me.'

He laughed: 'Don't they? It's very misleading. But once you know them – and they know that you know – well, you can have a good time with them. Just as long as you're not fooled. It's rather fun really.'

He looked at her golden head bent gracefully from her white neck: he loved to have her sitting there like that opposite him, sewing. She was wearing something soft and beige. He was vague about women's clothes and only knew what he liked and he liked this. 'Is that new?' he asked.

'Oh goodness, darling, you've seen it hundreds of times. … Why were they laughing? What did you say?'

'I just told them, in a roundabout way, that they were a pack of rogues.'

'And they like being told that?'

'If you say it in Hindustani, yes.'

'I *must* learn!'

'Yes you must,' he said without enthusiasm. 'It's the only language in which you can deliver deadly insults with the most flowery courtesy … I don't mean you, of course.' He laughed at the idea. 'What a shock they'd have!'

'Why? Mrs. Crawford speaks Hindustani; and Mrs. Minnies.'

'Yes but not with men. And they don't deliver deadly insults. It's a man's game, strictly.'

'What isn't?' Olivia said.

He sucked at his pipe in rather a pleased way which made her cry out sharply: 'Don't do that!' He took it out of his mouth and stared in surprise. 'I hate you with that thing, Douglas,' she explained.

Although he didn't understand why, he saw that she was upset so he laid it aside. 'I don't like it much myself,' he said frankly. There was a pause. She stopped sewing, stared into space; her pretty lower lip was

15 **tell sb. sth. in a roundabout way**: jdm. etwas auf Umwegen sagen
21 **courtesy**: politeness

sulky. He said 'It'll be all right once you get to the hills. It's the heat, darling, that's getting you.'

'I know it is ... but when will you be able to get away?'

'Never mind about me. It's you we have to take care of. I was talking to Beth today. They're thinking of leaving on the 17th, and I said kindly to book a berth for you at the same time. It's the Kalka Mail – an overnight journey, but it won't be too bad, I promise you.' He was so pleased with his arrangement that it did not occur to him she could be anything else. 'It's another four hours up the mountains but what a journey! You'll love it. The scenery, not to speak of the change of climate –'

'You don't for one moment think that I would go without you!'

'Beth Crawford will be there, and Mary Minnies. They'll take care of you.' He gave one look at her face and said 'That's just silly, Olivia. Mother spent four months away from Father every year for years on end. From April to September. She didn't like it either, but when you're in a district, that's the way it has to be.'

'I m not *going*,' Olivia said, sitting up very straight and looking at him very straight too. Then she said 'The Nawab wants to give a party for us.'

'Very kind of him,' Douglas said drily. He picked up his pipe again to knock it against the fender.

'Yes it is rather,' Olivia said. 'He sent Harry over specially to ask us.'

'It's not every day that royalty throws parties for junior officers.'

'No but I expect he's as bored as we are with our seniors.'

'*We* are?'

'*I* am.'

She was still looking at him straight but was weakened – not with fear but with love – by the way he was looking back at her. She had always loved his eyes. They were completely clear and unflinching – the eyes of a boy who read adventure stories and had dedicated himself to live up to their code of courage and honour.

1 **sulky**: silently bad-tempered 6 **berth**: bed on a boat or train **Kalka Mail**: name of an Indian train that runs to Kalka, a town near Simla 30 **unflinching**: firm and fearless 31 **dedicate yourself to sth.**: sich einer Sache widmen.

'Why are we quarrelling?' she asked.

He considered her question for a moment and then came up with his reasoned reply: 'Because the climate is making you irritable. That's only natural, it happens to all of us. And of course it's much worse for you having to stay home all day with nothing to do. That's why I want you to go away.' After a moment he added 'You don't think I like it any better than you, do you.'

Then she collapsed completely and could only be held up by his strong arms. She said she'd be bored, she'd be irritable, she'd be hot, she'd quarrel with him – all right! But please not to send her away from him.

The Nawab said 'When the guest will not grace the house of the host, then that house ceases to be a happy place.' Although this probably sounded better in Urdu, Olivia understood what he meant and felt both flattered and embarrassed.

'So I have come,' the Nawab said and spread his arms wide to show how much he was there.

He had come as before, with a whole retinue. But this time he refused to stay: he said no, it was his turn and he could not accept her hospitality again before she had accepted his. This embarrassed her more, for what could she tell him to explain her neglect of his invitations? But, like a man who understands every situation perfectly, he saw to it that she didn't have to explain anything. He told her that he had come all this way to invite her to a little drive and perhaps, if she felt like it, a little picnic somewhere in some shady spot? No, he could not – would not – be refused. The whole expedition need take only half an hour, fifteen minutes – let her look upon it only as a sort of *token* gesture, by way of reparation to him. He made it sound as if all sorts of intricate Indian

3 **irritable**: gereizt 12 **grace sth.**: give honour to sth.; to make sth. seem more attractive 13 **cease**: stop 15 **flatter sb.**: jdm. schmeicheln 18 **retinue**: Gefolge 21 **neglect** (n): act of giving too little attention or care to sb./sth. 27 **token gesture**: symbolische Geste 28 **reparation**: Entschädigung **intricate**: detailed and difficult to understand

codes of honour were involved – and perhaps they were, how was she to know? And she *wanted* to go so terribly!

He had come with two cars, a Rolls and an Alfa Romeo. All the young men with him piled into the Alfa Romeo while he himself, Olivia, and Harry sat in the Rolls. Harry was in front with the chauffeur. They drove past the Crawfords' house, past the Saunders', past the church and cemetery. Then they were out in open country. They drove on and on. The Nawab was sprawled next to her on the pearl-grey upholstery, one leg laid over the other, his arm flung carelessly along the back. He didn't say one word but smoked a great number of cigarettes. The country they drove through lay broiling in the sun. It glittered like glass and seemed to stretch out endlessly. At one point the Nawab reached across Olivia to pull down the blind on her window, as if wanting to spare her the sight of all that parched land. But it was all his land now: they had passed out of Satipur into his state of Khatm. No one said where they were going and Olivia felt foolish to ask. The Nawab's silence disturbed her. Was he bored, or in a bad mood? But in that case why had he insisted that she come? And now, having come, she felt as if she were in his power and had to submit to whatever mood he was in. Her dress stuck to the back of her legs with perspiration and she was afraid that, when she got out, it would be all wrinkled over the seat and look awful.

The car turned from the road and into a narrow track. It was difficult to drive here: they were shaken to and fro and Olivia hung on to the strap rather desperately so that she might not be flung against the Nawab. She was really very much afraid of this, for various mixed reasons. After a while the car couldn't go any further and they all had to get out and walk. The path got more and more narrow and climbed steeply upwards. The Nawab still didn't say anything though sometimes he held some branches aside to make it easier for Olivia to walk. But she still got scratched by thorns and also some insects were biting her; her straw hat had slipped to one side and she was very hot and near to tears. When she looked back, she saw Harry, also very hot, panting painfully behind

4 **pile into sth.**: in etwas hineindrängen 8 **sprawl**: lang ausstrecken **upholstery**: Sitzbezug 14 **parched**: dried out 25 **strap**: Gurt

them. The rest of their party was following them but at a respectful distance. The Nawab led the way, spotless in his white ducks and white-and-tan shoes.

He held aside some brambles and invited Olivia to walk ahead of him. They had arrived in a shady grove around a small stone shrine. It was cool and green here; there was even the sound of water. There was also a retinue of Palace servants who had already prepared the place for their entertainment. The ground had been spread with carpets and cushions on which Olivia was invited to recline. The Nawab and Harry joined her while the young men were sent off to amuse themselves elsewhere. The servants were busy unpacking hampers and cooling bottles of wine.

Now the Nawab became charming again. He apologised for the journey – 'Was it very horrid for you? Yes very horrid – oh our nasty Indian climate! I feel very very sorry for the inconvenience.'

'It's lovely here,' Olivia said, feeling terribly relieved: not only because she was cooler and more comfortable but because he was being nice again.

'It is a very special place,' the Nawab said. 'Wait, I will tell you, only first I think we must look after him: just see,' he said, indicating Harry who had flopped down on a rug with his arms extended and breathing rapidly in exhaustion. The Nawab laughed: 'What a state he is in. He is a very weak person. Because he is so flabby in his body I think. He is not a proper Englishman at all. No – shall I tell you – I think he is a very *im*proper Englishman.' He laughed at his joke and his eyes and teeth flashed; but at the same time he quite tenderly slipped a cushion under Harry's head. Harry groaned with his eyes shut: 'It's killing me.'

'What is killing you? This beautiful spot, sacred to my ancestors? Or perhaps it is our company?' He smiled at Olivia, then asked her 'Do you like it here? You don't mind I brought you? I wish Mr. Rivers would have come with us also. But I think Mr. Rivers must be very busy.'

2 **ducks** (pl): Segeltuchhosen 4 **bramble**: Dornenzweig 5 **grove**: Hain 9 **cushion**: Kissen 11 **hamper**: basket filled with food 15 **inconvenience**: Unannehmlichkeit 16 **relieved** [rɪ'li:vd]: erleichtert 21 **flop down**: move or fall in a loose and heavy way 23 **flabby**: soft and fat 28 **sacred** ['seɪkrɪd]: holy

He darted the tip of his tongue over his lips, then equally rapidly darted a look at Olivia: 'Mr. Rivers is a proper Englishman,' he declared.

'I know you like him,' Harry said from his prone position.

'Go to sleep! We are not talking with you but with each other … I think Mr. Rivers went to one of the English public schools? Eton or Rugby? Unfortunately I myself did not have this chance. If I have a son, I think I shall send him. What do you think? A very good education is to be obtained and also excellent discipline. Of course Harry did not like it at all, he says it is – what did you say it is, Harry?'

'Savage,' Harry said with feeling.

'What nonsense. Only for someone like you because you are improper. Let us try and make him a little bit proper, what do you think, Mrs. Rivers?' he said with another smile at her. He called to the young men who came running up and, at the Nawab's invitation, they threw themselves on Harry, and one massaged his legs and another his neck and a third tickled the soles of his feet. They all, including Harry, seemed to enjoy this game. The Nawab watched them, smiling indulgently, but when he saw Olivia was feeling left out, he turned to her and now he was again the way he had been with his guests at his dinner party: attentive, full of courtesy and consideration, making her feel that she was the only person there who mattered to him.

He invited her to see the shrine with him. It was a small plain whitewashed structure with a striped dome on top. Inside there were latticed windows to which people had tied bits of red thread, praying for fulfilment of their wishes. They had also laid strings of flowers – now wilted – on a little whitewashed mound that stood alone in the centre of the shrine. The Nawab explained that the shrine had been built by an ancestor of his in gratitude to Baba Firdaus who had lived on this spot. Baba Firdaus had been a devout soul devoted to prayer and solitude; the Nawab's ancestor – Amanullah Khan – had been a freebooter riding around the country with his own band of desperadoes to find what

1 **dart sth.**: move sth. quickly 3 **prone**: (here) horizontal 8 **obtain sth.**: get sth.
10 **savage**: uncivilized, brutal, primitive 16 **tickle sb./sth.**: jdn./etwas kitzeln
17 **indulgent**: nachsichtig 23 **striped**: gestreift **latticed** (adj): vergittert
26 **wilted** (adj): verwelkt **mound**: small hill 29 **devout**: very religious
solitude: state of being alone 30 **freebooter**: robber

pickings they could in the free-for-all between Moghuls, Afghans, Mahrattas, and the East India Company. In the course of a long career, he had had a lot of ups and downs. Once he had sought refuge in this grove – all his men had been killed in an engagement, and he himself had only just escaped with his life, though badly wounded. Baba Firdaus had kept him hidden from his pursuers and also tended his wounds and nursed him back to health. Years later, when fortune smiled on him again, Amanullah Khan had returned; but by then the place was deserted and no one knew what had happened to the Baba, or even whether he was dead or alive. So all Amanullah Khan could do was to build this little shrine in the holy man's honour.

'Because he never forgot friend or foe', the Nawab said about his ancestor. 'Where there was a score to be settled for good or bad, he did not forget. He was only a rough soldier but very straight and honourable. And a great fighter. The British liked him very much. I think you always like such people?' He looked enquiringly at Olivia. She laughed – it seemed strange to her to be nominated as a spokesman for the British. Then he smiled too: 'Yes you like rough people who fight well and are mostly on a horse. Best of all you like the horse. But I think you don't like others so much?'

'What others?' Olivia asked, laughing.

'For instance,' he said, also laughing, 'myself.' But then he grew serious and said 'But you are a different type of person. You don't like horses, I think? No. Come here please, I will show you something.'

He led her out of the shrine. There was a little spring which came freshly bubbling out of a cleft between some stones. It was the sound of this spring that, together with the bird-song, filled that green grove. The Nawab squatted down and dabbled his fingers in the water and invited

1 **pickings** (pl): Beute **free-for-all** (infml): struggle to gain power or influence **Moghuls**: the Muslim rulers of much of India from the 16th to 18th centuries
2 **Mahrattas** (usu. **Marathas**): members of a Hindu state that was powerful in the 18th century **the East India Company**: British trading company that dominated Indian affairs in the 18th and 19th centuries 4 **engagement**: small battle
6 **pursuer**: Verfolger 8 **deserted**: left empty 12 **foe**: enemy 16 **enquiring** (adj): as if asking a question, curious 26 **cleft**: Spalte 28 **dabble sth.**: move sth. (esp. your hands or feet) playfully about (in water)

Olivia to do the same: 'How cold it is. It is always like that. People think it is a miracle that there should be this green grove and this cold water here in this place where there is only desert. Why is it so? Some say it is because of Baba Firdaus and his holy life, others say because Amanullah Khan paid his debt of gratitude. Do you believe that it could be so? That there is a miracle?'

They were side by side. He looked at her intensely and she looked down at her hands which she was dabbling in the water. It was fresh and fast running but so shallow that it just trickled over her fingers. She said 'Perhaps a very small miracle.'

Then he slapped his knee and laughed loudly: 'Oh Mrs. Rivers you have a good sense of humour!' He got up and held out his hand solicitously though she managed without him. 'Do you know,' he said then, very serious again, 'that as soon as I saw you I knew you would be this type of person? Shall I tell you something? It is very funny: I feel I can tell you anything, anything at all, and you will understand. It is very rare to have this feeling with another person. But with you I have it. And something else also: I'm not someone who believes very much in miracles, not at all. I'm too scientific to have such beliefs. But also I think that there are things that *could* be, even if they are miracles. Don't you think so? That this could be? Ah, you see: I knew. You are much more the same type like myself than like – for instance – for instance – Mrs. Crawford.' He laughed, she laughed. He looked into her eyes. 'You are not at all like Mrs. Crawford,' he said while doing this; but next moment he saw he was embarrassing her so he smilingly released her from his intense gaze and, very gently just touching her elbow, propelled her back to where the others were.

Now he was in an excellent mood and the party began to go with a swing. The servants had unpacked the picnic hampers, filling the sacred grove with roasted chickens, quails, and potted shrimps. The young men were very lively and entertained sometimes with practical jokes which they played on each other, and sometimes with songs and Urdu

12–13 **solicitous**: caring 26 **gaze**: long look **propel sb./sth.**: push or move sb./sth. forward 30 **quail**: Wachtel **potted shrimps**: shrimps which have been cooked and preserved in butter

verses. One of them had brought a lute-like instrument out of which he plucked some bittersweet notes. The lute also provided the music for the game of musical chairs they played, with cushions laid in a row. It happened – whether by accident or design Olivia didn't know – that she and the Nawab were the last two players left. Very, very slowly they circled around the one remaining cushion, keeping their eyes on each other, each alert to what the other might do next. Everyone watched, the lute played. For a moment she thought that, as an act of courtesy, he was going to let her win; but quite suddenly – he heard the music stop before she did – he flung himself on the one remaining cushion. He had won! He laughed out loud and threw up both his arms in triumph. He was really tremendously pleased.

* * * *

8 March. It is from this time on that Olivia's letters to Marcia really begin. She had been writing to her before that, but infrequently and not in great detail: and it is only from the day of the Nawab's picnic that she began to write as if it were a relief to have someone to confide in.

Olivia never told Douglas about the Nawab's picnic. She had meant to as soon as she got home, but it so happened that he had been held up by a stabbing incident in the bazaar that day and was even later than usual. She asked him many questions, and as he loved talking about his work (she wasn't always all that interested), the time just went and she never did get round to telling him about her day. And when he left next morning, she was still asleep. So instead she wrote the first of her long letters to Marcia. I wonder what Marcia can have made of these letters: she was living in France at the time – she had married a Frenchman but they had separated and Marcia was on her own, living in a series of hotel rooms and getting involved with some rather difficult people. Olivia's life in India must have seemed strange and far-off.

1 **lute**: Laute 2 **pluck sth.**: etwas zupfen **notes** (pl): Töne, Klang 7 **alert**: watchful 12 **tremendously**: exceptionally, very 16 **confide in sb.**: tell sb. about your private matters 19 **stab sb.**: push a knife into sb. 26 **separate from sb.**: stop living together with sb.

I have laid Olivia's letters out on my little desk and work on them and on this journal throughout the morning. My day in Satipur has taken on a steady routine. It starts early because the town wakes early. First there are the temple bells – I lie in bed and listen to them – and then the fire is lit and the kettle put on in the tea-stall opposite. The air is fresh at this hour of the morning, the sky tender and pale. Everything seems as harmonious as the temple bells. I go down to the bazaar to buy curds and fresh green vegetables, and after cooking my meal, I settle down crosslegged on the floor to work on my papers.

Towards evening I sometimes go to the post office which is situated in what used to be Olivia's breakfast room. If it is about the time when the offices close, I walk over to the Crawfords' house to wait for Inder Lal. Both houses – the Crawfords' and Olivia's – once so different in their interiors are now furnished with the same ramshackle office furniture, and also have the same red betel stains on their walls. Their gardens too are identical now – that is, they are no longer gardens but patches of open ground where the clerks congregate in the shade of whatever trees have been left. Pedlars have obtained licences to sell peanuts and grams. There are rows of cycle stands with a cycle jammed into every notch.

It used to embarrass Inder Lal to find me waiting for him. Perhaps he was even a little ashamed to be seen with me. I suppose we do make a strange couple – I'm so much taller than he is, and I walk with long strides and keep forgetting that this makes it difficult for him to keep up with me. But I think by now he has got used to me and perhaps is even rather proud to be seen walking with his English friend. I also think he quite likes my company now. At first he welcomed it mainly to practise his English – he said it was a very good chance for him – but now he also seems to enjoy our conversations. I certainly do. He is very frank with me and tells me all sorts of personal things: not only about his life

6 **tender**: soft, gentle 8 **curds** (pl): Quark 14 **ramshackle**: old and in a bad state 15 **betel (leaf)**: type of leaf that is chewed and turns red **stain**: Flecken 17 **congregate**: meet, come together 18 **pedlar**: person who travels from house to house to sell small articles 19 **grams**: Kichererbsen 20 **notch**: Fahrradhalterung 24 **stride**: step 29 **frank**: honest and open

but also about his feelings. He has told me that the only other person he can talk to freely is his mother but even with her – well, he said, with the mother there are certain things one cannot speak as with the friend.

Once I asked 'What about your wife?'

He said she was not intelligent. Also she had not had much education – his mother had not wanted him to marry a very educated girl; she said there was nothing but trouble to be expected from such a quarter. Ritu had been chosen on account of her suitable family background and her fair complexion. His mother had told him she was pretty, but he never could make up his mind about that. Sometimes he thought yes, sometimes no. He asked my opinion. I said yes. She must have been so when young, though now she is thin and worn and her face, like his, always anxious.

He told me that during the first years of her marriage she had been so homesick that she had never stopped crying. 'It was very injurious to her health,' he said, 'especially when she got in family way. Mother and I tried to explain matters to her, how it was necessary for her to eat and be happy, but she did not understand. Naturally her health suffered and the child also was born weak. It was her fault. An intelligent person would have understood and taken care.'

He frowned and looked unhappy. By this time we had reached the lake. (This is about as far as Olivia would have got if she ever ventured to this side: because beyond this point the Indian part of the town began, the crowded lanes and bazaar where I now live.)

Inder Lal said 'How is it possible for me to talk with her the way I am now talking with you? It is not possible. She would understand nothing.' He added: 'Her health also has remained very weak.'

There were some boys swimming in the lake. They seemed to be having a very good time. We could see the water rising in sprays as they jumped up and down and splashed one another. Inder Lal watched them wistfully. Perhaps he wished he were one of them; or he may have

7 **quarter**: (here) type 8 **on account of**: because of 9 **fair complexion**: helle Hautfarbe 12 **worn** (adj): looking very tired 15 **injurious**: schädlich 16 **get in (the) family way** (infml): pregnant 21 **frown**: die Stirn runzeln 22 **venture**: dare to go 31 **wistful**: thinking sadly about sth. you would like

been remembering summer evenings of his own when he too had gone swimming with his friends.

It could not have been all that long ago – he is still a young man, a few years younger than I am, about 25 or 26. When you look closer, you can see that his face really is young, only he seems older because of his careworn expression. When I first saw him, he seemed to me a typical Indian clerk, meek and bowed down with many cares. But now I see that he is not meek and bowed at all – or only outwardly – that really inside himself he is alive and yearning for all sorts of things beyond his reach. It shows mainly in his eyes which are beautiful – full of melancholy and liquid with longing.

10 March. I work hard at my Hindi and am beginning to have conversations with people which is a great advantage. I wish I could talk more with Ritu, Inder Lal's wife, but she is so shy that my improved Hindi doesn't help me with her at all. Although I'm quite a shy person myself, I try not to be with her. I feel it is my responsibility to get us going since I'm older and (I think) stronger. There is something frail, *weak* about her. Physically she is very thin, with thin arms on which her bangles slip about; but not only physically – I have the impression that her mind, or do I mean her will, is not strong either, that she is the sort of person who would give way quickly. Sometimes she tries to overcome her shyness and pays me a visit in my room; but though I talk away desperately in my appalling Hindi just so she will stay, quite soon she jumps up and runs away. The same happens when I try to visit her – I've seen her at my approach run to hide in the bathroom and, though it is not very salubrious (the little sweeper girl is not too good at her job), stay locked up in there till I go away again.

The days – and nights – are really heating up now. It is unpleasant to sleep indoors and everyone pulls out their beds at night. The town has

6 **careworn**: worried 7 **meek**: quiet and gentle 9 **yearn for sb./sth.**: long for sb./sth. 11 **liquid**: (hier) feucht 17 **frail**: physically weak 19 **bangle**: large ring worn by Indian women as jewellery round the arm **slip about**: hin und her rutschen 23 **appalling** (adj): very bad 25 **approach** (n): Näherkommen 26 **salubrious** (fml): clean and healthy

become a communal dormitory. There are string-beds in front of all the stalls, and on the roofs, and in the courtyards: wherever there is an open space. I kept on sleeping indoors for a while since I was embarrassed to go to bed in public. But it just got too hot, so now I too have dragged my bed out into the courtyard and have joined it on to the Inder Lals' line. The family of the shop downstairs also sleep in this courtyard, and so does their little servant boy, and some others I haven't been able to identify. So we're quite a crowd. I no longer change into a nightie but sleep, like an Indian woman, in a sari.

It's amazing how *still* everything is. When Indians sleep, they really do sleep. Neither adults nor children have a regular bed-time – when they're tired they just drop, fully clothed, on to their beds, or the ground if they have no beds, and don't stir again till the next day begins. All one hears is occasionally someone crying out in their sleep, or a dog – maybe a jackal – baying at the moon. I lie awake for hours: with happiness, actually. I have never known such a sense of communion. Lying like this under the open sky there is a feeling of being immersed in space – though not in empty space, for there are all these people sleeping all around me, the whole town and I am part of it. How different from my often very lonely room in London with only my own walls to look at and my books to read.

A few nights ago there was such a strange sound – for a moment I didn't react but lay there just *hearing* it: a high-pitched wail piercing through the night. It didn't seem like a human sound. But it was. By the time I had sat up, Inder Lal's mother had got to Ritu's bed and was holding her hand over the girl's mouth. Ritu struggled but the mother was stronger. No one else had stirred yet and the mother was desperately holding on. I helped her get Ritu into the house, and when I turned on the light, I saw Ritu's eyes stretched wide in fear above the mother's

1 **communal dormitory**: room in which many people sleep **string-bed**: type of bed with strips of fabric have been tied across a frame 8 **nightie**: nightdress
13 **stir**: move 15 **jackal**: Schakal **bay**: bark deeply and repeatedly; howl
16 **sense of communion**: feeling of being part of the universe 17 **be immersed in sth.**: be completely covered by sth. 23 **high-pitched wail**: loud, high cry
pierce sth.: etwas durchdringen.

hand still laid over her mouth. When those strange sounds had completely stopped, the mother released her and she sank at once to the floor and remained hunched up there with her face buried in her knees. Now she was quite still except for occasional spasms that twitched through her little bird body. The mother went to the jars where the rice was stored and scattered a handful over Ritu's head. The grains bounced off the girl's hair though one or two got stuck there. She still didn't move. The mother opened and closed her hand and circled it over that bowed head, cracking her knuckles, and she was also murmuring some incantation. Quite soon Ritu got up, looking tear-stained and exhausted but otherwise normal. The three of us went out again and lay back on our beds next to the others who hadn't moved. Next day neither the mother nor Ritu mentioned the incident, so that it might just not have been except that there were some rice grains stuck in Ritu's hair.

20 March. After that night the mother and I have drawn closer together. We have become friends. Now she often accompanies me to the bazaar and bullies the shopkeeper if he is not giving me the best vegetables. She has seen to it that everyone charges me the right price. I understand her Hindi much better now, and she some of mine though it still makes her laugh. But she does most of the talking and I like listening to her, especially when she tells me about herself. I have the impression that, although she is a widow, the best part of her life is now. She does not seem to have a high opinion of married life. She has told me that the first years are always difficult because of being so homesick and thinking only of the father's house: and it is difficult to get used to the new family and to the rule of the mother-in-law. She rarely mentions her late husband so I presume he didn't make up for much. But she seems to be very close to her son – it is she, not Ritu, who does everything for him like serving his food and laying his clothes out. She is very proud of him for being a government servant and working in an office instead of

3 **hunched up**: gekrümmt 4 **spasm**: Krampf **twitch**: zucken 5 **jar**: container for storing food 6 **grain**: (Reis)korn 9 **knuckle**: (Finger)knöchel
10 **incantation**: words used as a magic spell **tear-stained**: red from crying
17 **bully sb.**: force sb. to do sth. by frightening them 27 **presume sth.**: etwas vermuten

sitting in a shop like his father used to do (he was a grocer). It is a great step up for him and so for her too. She certainly holds her head high when she walks through the town. She is about fifty but strong and healthy and full of feminine vigour. Unlike Ritu, she doesn't spend all her time at home but has outings with her friends who are mostly healthy widows like herself. They roam around town quite freely and don't care at all if their saris slip down from their heads or even from their breasts. They gossip and joke and giggle like schoolgirls: very different from their daughters-in-law who are sometimes seen shuffling behind them, heavily veiled and silent and with the downcast eyes of prisoners under guard.

Since we started getting friendly, Inder Lal's mother invites me along on some of her jaunts. I've been introduced to all her friends, including a sort of leader they have – another widow whom they call 'Maji' though she is not that much older than they are. Maji is said to have certain powers, and though I don't know what they are, she does give me the impression of having something more than other people, even if it is only more vim and vigour. She seems to be positively bursting with those. She lives very simply in a little hut under a tree. It is a lovely spot, in between the lake where the boys go swimming and a lot of old royal tombs. When I was taken to see her, we all crawled inside her hut and sat on the mud floor there. I enjoyed being with all those widows, they were so gay and friendly, and though I couldn't take much part in their conversation, I did a lot of smiling and nodding; and when they all began to sing hymns – led by Maji who sang very lustily, throwing herself around in her enthusiasm – I tried to join in which seemed to please them.

After that Inder Lal's mother took me to see the suttee shrines. We walked to the end of the bazaar and through the gateway leading out of

4 **vigour**: energy, vitality 5 **outing**: short trip 6 **roam**: walk without any definite aim 9 **shuffle**: schlurfen 10 **veiled** (adj): verschleiert 13 **jaunt**: short trip for pleasure 14 **maji** (Hindi): mother 18 **vim** (old-fashioned): Schwung, Elan **burst with sth.**: vor etwas platzen 21 **tomb**: small building in which a person is buried 25 **lustily** (adv): kraftvoll 28 **suttee**: A custom in which wives throw themselves onto the flames that burn their dead husbands. As these suttee widows were considered virtuous and honourable, small shrines (i.e. places of worship) were created for them.

town, then down a dusty road till we came to a tank or reservoir by the wayside. Here Inder Lal's mother showed me a cluster of little shrines under some trees: they were not much bigger than mile-stones, though some of them had little domes on top. There were crude figures scratched hair-thin into the stone: presumably the husband with the faithful wife who had burned herself with him. They gave me an eerie feeling, but Inder Lal's mother devoutly joined her hands before the shrines. She decorated one of them with a little string of roses and marigolds she had brought. She told me that, on certain days of the year, she and her friends come with sweets, milk, and flowers to worship these widows who have made the highest sacrifice. She sounded really respectful and seemed to have the greatest reverence for that ancient custom. She even seemed regretful – this merry widow! – that it had been discontinued (it was outlawed in 1829). She showed me the shrine of the last suttee which of course I knew about as it had taken place during Olivia's time. Although this shrine only dates back to 1923, it looks as age-old as the others.

1923

It had happened when Mr. Crawford was away on tour and Douglas on his own in charge of the district. A grain merchant had died and his widow had been forced by her relatives to burn herself with him on his funeral pyre. Although Douglas had rushed to the scene the moment information reached him, he had arrived too late to save the woman. All he could still do was arrest the main instigators who were her sons, brothers-in-law, and a priest. Everyone praised Douglas for the calm and competent way he had handled the situation. Even the Nawab made a point of congratulating him – though Douglas received *those* congratulations rather coldly. But the Nawab did not notice or, if he did, was not put out.

4 **crude**: not completed in much detail 6 **eerie** ['ɪəri]: causing fear because sth. is strange 9 **marigold**: Ringelblume 11 **sacrifice** (n): Opfer 12 **reverence for sb./sth.**: feeling of deep respect or admiration for sb./sth. 14 **outlaw sth.**: make sth. illegal 22 **funeral pyre**: Scheiterhaufen 24 **instigator**: person who provokes or begins sth. that is considered bad 29 **be put out** (infml): be upset

Olivia had still not told Douglas about the Nawab's picnic; nor about the Nawab's subsequent visits – he came almost every second or third day now, usually with all his companions. Not that she didn't want to tell Douglas – of course she did! – but he was always home so late and then with so many preoccupations of his own, she never seemed to have an opportunity to tell him. However, one day the Nawab lingered on till Douglas' arrival home. He must have deliberately planned to do so because that day he had left all his young men behind. If Olivia was nervous about this meeting, she need not have been because the Nawab handled it perfectly. He sprang to his feet to receive Douglas and held out his hand in hearty English greeting. It was as if he were the host and this his house in which it was his duty to make Douglas welcome. He said at once that his purpose in driving over that day was to congratulate Douglas on his prompt action. When Douglas, cool and deprecating, said he wished he had been prompt enough to get there before rather than after the event, the Nawab shrugged in commiseration:

'What is to be done, Mr. Rivers. These people will never learn. Whatever we do, they will still cling to their barbaric customs. But, Mr. Rivers, what praise there is for you everywhere! On your conduct of this miserable affair, all speak as one.'

'You are misinformed,' Douglas said. 'There's been a lot of murmuring. It seems my prisoners – the unfortunate woman's relatives – are in some quarters regarded as martyrs. We even had a bit of trouble outside the jail today.' He gave Olivia a quick, sharp look: 'You are not to worry. Nothing we couldn't easily handle.'

'Of course you need not at all worry, Mrs. Rivers!' the Nawab likewise assured her. 'Where Mr. Rivers is, there is firm control and strong action. As there must be. Otherwise these people cannot be managed at all. All must be grateful to you, Mr. Rivers, for your strong hand,' he said, looking at Douglas man-to-man and not seeming to notice that Douglas did not look back at him that way. As soon as Mr. Crawford returned

5 **preoccupation**: Beschäftigung, Sorge 6 **linger on**: stay 7 **deliberate**: intentional 14 **deprecating** (adj): missbilligend 16 **shrug**: raise your shoulders slightly **commiseration**: sympathy 18 **cling to sth.**: stick to sth. 19 **conduct of sth.**: way of managing sth.

from tour, he gave a dinner party at which the main topic of conversation was again the suttee. Douglas came in for much praise. Although embarrassed – he played furiously with his piece of Melba toast – he was also proud, for he highly respected his superiors and set great store by their good opinion of him. Besides Douglas and Olivia, the other guests were the Minnies and Dr. Saunders (Mrs. Saunders not well enough to come): in fact, the same people as usual, there being no other English officers in the district. The meal also was as usual – the bland, soggy food the Crawfords might have eaten at home except that their Indian cook had somehow taken it a soggy stage further. However, the way it was served, by bearers in turbans and cummerbunds, was rather grand. So were the plate and silver: they had been handed down to Mrs Crawford by her grandmother who had bought them in Calcutta, at an auction of the effects of an English merchant-banker gone bankrupt.

After discussing this particular case of suttee, the diners went on to remember past incidents of the same nature. These were drawn not so much from personal experience as from a rich store-house of memories that went back several generations and was probably interesting to those who shared it. The only person there besides Olivia who did not was Dr. Saunders. He concentrated on his dinner though from time to time he contributed exasperated exclamations. The others, however, told their anecdotes with no moral comment whatsoever, even though they had to recount some hair-raising events. And not only did they keep completely cool, but they even had that little smile of tolerance, of affection, even enjoyment that Olivia was beginning to know well: like good parents, they all loved India whatever mischief she might be up to.

'Mind you,' said Major Minnies, 'there *have* been cases of wives who actually did want to be burned with their husbands.'

'Don't believe a word of it!' from Dr. Saunders.

3 **Melba toast**: type of thin toast 4–5 **set great store by sb./sth.**: lay great value on sth. 8 **bland**: without much taste 9 **soggy**: completely wet 11 **bearer**: servant who carries things **cummerbund**: broad belt of cloth worn round a man's waist at formal occasions 14 **effects** (pl): belongings 21 **exasperated** (adj): verärgert 23 **recount sth.**: tell sth. 26 **mischief**: bad behaviour

'I don't think your suttee lady was an altogether willing participant,' Mr. Crawford twinkled at Douglas.

'No,' said Douglas, holding in a lot more.

Olivia looked across at him and said 'How do you know?' It was like a challenge and she meant it to be. He hadn't talked to her much about the suttee, wanting to spare her the details (which were indeed very painful – he was to hear that woman's screams to the end of his days). But Olivia resented being spared. 'It's part of their religion, isn't it? I thought one wasn't supposed to meddle with that.' Now she looked down into her Windsor soup and not at all at Douglas; but she went on stubbornly: 'And quite apart from religion, it is their culture and who are we to interfere with anyone's culture especially an ancient one like theirs.'

'Culture!' cried Dr. Saunders. 'You've been talking to that bounder Horsham!' Olivia didn't know it but her words had recalled those of an English member of Parliament who had passed through the district the year before and had put everyone's back up.

But Dr. Saunders and Douglas were the only ones to be annoyed with Olivia. The others sportingly discussed her point of view as if it were one that could be taken seriously. They spoke of the sanctity of religious practices, even took into account the possibility of voluntary suttee: but came to the conclusion that, when all was said and done, it was still suicide and in a particularly gruesome form.

'I know,' Olivia said miserably. She had no desire to recommend widow-burning but it was everyone else being so sure – tolerant and smiling but *sure* – that made her want to take another stand. 'But in theory it is really, isn't it, a *noble* idea. In theory,' she pleaded. Without daring to glance in Douglas' direction, she knew him to be sitting very upright with his thin lips held in tight and his eyes cold. She went on

2 **twinkle**: mit einem Augenzwinkern sagen 8 **resent sth.**: feel anger about sth. 9 **meddle with sth.**: interfere in sth. that is not your concern 10 **Windsor soup**: type of brown meat and vegetable soup 11 **stubborn**: störrisch 14 **bounder** (old use, infml): man who behaves badly and cannot be trusted 17 **put sb.'s back up**: annoy sb. 19 **sporting**: fair and generous 20 **sanctity**: state of being holy 23 **gruesome**: cruel 27 **plead**: make a point strongly in a begging way

rather desperately: 'I mean, to want to go with the person you care for most in the world. Not to want to be alive any more if he wasn't.'

'It's savagery,' Dr. Saunders declared. 'Like everything else in this country, plain savagery and barbarism. I've seen some sights in my hospital I wouldn't like to tell you about, not with ladies present I wouldn't. Most gruesome and horrible mutilations – and all, mind you, in the name of religion. If this is religion, then by gad!' he said, so loudly and strongly that the old head-bearer with the hennaed beard trembled from head to foot, 'I'd be proud to call myself an atheist.'

But Major Minnies – perhaps out of gallantry – rallied to Olivia's side with an anecdote that partly bore out her point of view. It was not something that had happened to him personally but a hundred years earlier and to Colonel Sleeman when in charge of the district of Jabalpore. Sleeman had tried to prevent a widow from committing suttee but had been defeated by her determination to perish together with her husband's corpse.

'That really was a voluntary suttee,' Major Minnies told Olivia. 'Her sons and the rest of her family joined Colonel Sleeman in attempting to prevent her, but it was no use. She was determined. She sat for four days on a rock in the river and said that if she wasn't allowed to burn herself then she'd starve herself to death. In any case she wasn't going to be left behind. In the end Sleeman had to give way – yes he lost that round but I'll tell you something – he speaks of the old lady with respect. She wasn't a fanatic, she wasn't even very dramatic about it, she just sat there quietly and waited and said no, she wanted to go with her husband. There was something noble there,' said the Major – and now he wasn't being tolerant and amused, not in the least.

'Too noble for me, I fear,' said Beth Crawford – as hostess, she probably felt it was time to change the tone. 'Fond as I am of you, dear man,' she told her husband across the table, 'I don't really think I could –'

3 **savagery**: primitive cruelty 6 **mutilation**: Verstümmelung 7 **by gad** (old use): by God 8 **head-bearer**: senior servant **hennaed** (adj): coloured with henna 10 **gallantry**: good manners **rally to sb.'s side**: support sb. 15 **perish**: die 16 **corpse**: dead body 23 **round**: (here) particular struggle

'Oh I could!' cried Olivia, and with such feeling that everyone was silent and looked at her. Douglas also looked – and this time she dared raise her eyes to his: even if he was angry with her. 'I'd want to. I mean, I just wouldn't want to go on living. I'd be *grateful* for such a custom.'

Their eyes met across the table. She saw his hard look melt away into tenderness. And she felt the same way towards him. Her feelings became so strong that she could not go on looking into his eyes. She looked down at her plate, meekly began to cut the hard piece of chicken in floury sauce that had replaced the hard piece of fried fish of the preceding course: and thought that really everything was quite easy to bear and overcome just as long as she and Douglas felt the way they did for each other.

* * * *

30 March. I had to go to the post office so afterwards I waited as usual to go home with Inder Lal. We had got as far as the royal tombs – near the lake and Maji's hut – when we heard some strange sounds coming out of one of them. They seemed like groans. Inder Lal said 'It is better to go home.' But when we reached the next tomb – there is a whole cluster of them, all of one 14th century royal family – we again heard the same sound coming from behind us. It *was* a groan. Despite Inder Lal's protests, I turned back to investigate. I ascended the steps; although these tombs have no side-walls but are closed in by arches and lattices, they are very dark inside. At first all I could make out was the vague mass of the sarcophagi in the centre: but when the groaning noise was repeated, I noticed that it came from another shape huddled in one corner. This was human and dressed in something orange. I went up close – Inder Lal gave a warning shout from outside – and got down to peer at the groaner. I recognised him as the white sadhu, Chid, whom I had once met outside the travellers' rest-house.

16 **groan**: deep sound made when in pain 20 **ascend**: go up 21 **arch**: Gewölbe
23 **sarcophagus** (pl **sarcophagi** [sɑːˈkɒfəgaɪ]): Steinsarg 24 **be huddled**: kauern
27 **peer at sb./sth.**: look at sb./sth. **sadhu** (Hindi): holy or wise man

He had all his possessions with him – a bundle, an umbrella, prayer-beads, and a begging bowl – and they were scattered around him where he lay propped against a latticed arch. There were also some bits of dried bun on a newspaper. He said he didn't know how long he had been lying here – sometimes it was dark and sometimes it was darker, he said. He had been thrown out of the travellers' rest-house when his two companions had moved on. He had then tried to continue his pilgrimage, but feeling very ill on the road, had dragged himself back to Satipur. He said he was still very ill. He had been lying here alone, and no one had bothered him because no one had found him except once a pariah dog had sniffed at him and gone away again.

Inder Lal, standing inside an arch at a cautious distance, warned me 'Be careful.'

'It's all right,' I said. 'It's someone I know.' I felt Chid's forehead and found it to be hot.

He groaned: 'I'm thirsty … and hungry,' he added, patting his stomach hard like an Indian beggar so one could hear the hollow sound.

Inder Lal had now come up cautiously and stood looking down at Chid: 'Why is he dressed like that?' he asked.

'He is a sadhu,' I explained.

'How can he be sadhu?'

'He's studied Hindu religion.'

It was horrible inside the tomb – there was an acrid smell of bat droppings and also I think Chid must have been disrespectful enough to use the place as a lavatory. I wondered what to do with him: he couldn't be left, but where should I take him?

'What has he studied?' Inder Lal asked; he was now keenly interested. 'What have you studied?' he probed. 'Do you know the Puranas? What about the Brahmanas?'

3 **propped up**: supported (by sth.) 8 **pilgrimage**: Wallfahrt **drag yourself**: move slowly and with effort 11 **pariah dog** [pə'raɪə]: streunender Hund 16 **pat sb./sth.**: tap sb./sth. with the open hand 17 **hollow**: empty 24 **acrid smell**: strong bitter smell **bat**: Fledermaus 25 **dropping**: Kot 29 **probe**: ask sb. questions to make them tell things that are personal or secret **Puranas**: sacred poems written in Sanskrit 30 **Brahmanas**: Hindu scriptures

Chid did not hear these questions; he was looking at me with pleading, fevered eyes. 'Do you live near?' he asked me. 'I could walk if it's *very* near.'

I was reluctant, but Inder Lal seemed to fancy the idea of taking Chid home with us.

10 April. Although Chid recovered from his fever after a few days, he has given no indication of leaving. I suppose it is restful for him in my room after all his travelling across India. It is not very restful for me though. I have had to lock up all my papers – Olivia's letters and this journal – not because I mind his reading them (I don't think he'd be very interested anyway) but because of the way he ruffled through them and left them scattered about with dirty finger-marks on them. These finger-marks are on everything in my room now. He makes no secret of going through my possessions and taking whatever he needs: in fact, he has explained to me that he doesn't believe in possessions and thinks it is bad for people to be attached to them. He is not very demanding, actually – he eats the food I prepare and is satisfied with everything he is given. He spends a lot of time walking around town and has become a familiar figure so that even the children have got tired of running after him. Some of the shopkeepers allow him to sit in their stalls with them and occasionally he collects quite a crowd as he sits there crosslegged and expounds his philosophy.

Everyone considers it a privilege for me to have him in my room. It seems I have been presented with an excellent opportunity to acquire merit by serving a holy man in charity. The question as to whether Chid is holy may remain open, but as far as the town is concerned, he has made a promising first step in shaving his head and throwing away his clothes. For this they seem ready to give him the benefit of many doubts. I've seen them do the same with Indian holy men who often pass through the town with their ochre robes and beads and begging bowls.

4 **reluctant**: zögerlich 7 **restful**: relaxing 11 **ruffle through sth.**: look through sth. and mix it all up 16 **be attached to sb./sth.**: an jdm./etwas hängen 22 **expound sth.**: explain sth. in detail 25 **merit**: reward **charity**: Nächstenliebe. Wohltätigkeit 30 **ochre** ['əʊkə]: ockerfarben

On the whole they look a sturdy set of rascals to me – some of them heavily drugged, others randy as can be, all it seems to me with shrewd and greedy faces. But as they pass through the streets, some half naked, some fully so, rapping their pilgrim staffs and shouting out the name of God as pedlars shout their wares, people come running out of their houses to lay offerings into the ready begging bowls. Chid also has a begging bowl and often people put something in it – a banana or a guava – which he eats by himself in a corner of my room, afterwards leaving the peel on the floor. When I tell him to pick it up, he does so quite meekly.

Inder Lal is much impressed with Chid. As soon as he comes home from the office, he climbs up to my room and sits there for hours listening to Chid. Chid tells him about the centres of energy within the body and the methods to be employed in order to release them. He points now to his skull and now contorts himself so as to dig himself in the base of his spine; and then he weaves his hands about in the air as if drawing down spiritual forces to be found there. I get very bored with all this. It seems to me that Chid has picked up scraps of spiritual and religious lore here and there, and as he is neither an intelligent nor very educated boy, it has all sort of fermented inside him and makes him sound a bit mad at times. Perhaps he is a bit mad.

I still don't know anything about him. Sometimes he gives me accounts of himself, but they are always different and it is impossible to reconcile one with another. Anyway, as they deal mostly with the development of his spiritual life, they are abstract rather than personal. Inder Lal tells me this is quite all right because Chid has no personal past. When someone becomes a Hindu ascetic, all his former life – indeed, his former lives – everything he has ever thought or done or been is burned up: literally burned up, for a funeral pyre is lit and the aspirant's

1 **sturdy**: fit and healthy **rascal** (old-fashioned): dishonest and bad person 2 **randy**: full of sexual desire **shrewd**: bösartig, hinterlistig 4 **rap sth.**: strike sth. quickly and lightly **pilgrim staff**: Pilgerstab 15 **contort sth.**: etwas verrenken/verdrehen 16 **spine**: Wirbelsäule 18 **scrap**: small piece, bit 19 **lore** (old-fashioned): knowledge 20 **ferment**: gären 24 **reconcile with sth.**: find agreement between sth (e.g. two ideas or situations that seem to be in opposition) 29 **aspirant**: (here) person who wants to achieve sth.

clothes and shaved hair consumed in it in a symbolic cremation. Chid has undergone this ceremony, so that now, according to Inder Lal, he is nothing but the Hindu sadhu we see before us. However, he has retained his flat Midlands accent which makes everything he says even more weird.

He is always hungry, and not only for food. He also needs sex very badly and seems to take it for granted that I will give it to him the same way I give him my food. I have never had such a feeling of being used. In fact, he admits that this is what he is doing – using me to reach a higher plane of consciousness through the powers of sex that we are engendering between us. I don't really know why I let him go ahead. I'm much bigger and stronger than he is and could easily keep him off. But it seems as if there really is something, some emanation, that does not come from him but from some powers outside himself. Because he himself is quite sexless: his cheeks are smooth except for some scattered tufts of blonde hair, and he is terribly skinny like a boy who has just got up from a sickbed. But he has constant erections and goes to a tremendous size, so that I am reminded of the Lord Shiva whose huge member is worshipped by devout Hindu women. At such times it seems to me that his sex is engendered by his spiritual practices, by all that chanting of mantras he does sitting beads in hand on the floor of my room.

15 April. Typical of the way things get mixed up in India is the story of Baba Firdaus' shrine. As the Nawab had explained to Olivia, this had originally been built by his ancestor Amanullah Khan in thanksgiving to a Muslim faqir who had given him shelter. It is now sacred to Hindu women because it is thought that offerings at this shrine will cure

1 **cremation**: act of burning a dead body 5 **weird** [wɪəd]: strange 7 **take sth. for granted**: assume sth. to be normal 10 **plane**: level 11 **engender sth.**: generate sth., create sth. 13 **emanation**: Ausströmen 18 **Lord Shiva**: one of the most important Hindu gods, the god of 'destruction' 19 **member**: penis 21 **chant**: sing words continuously in a repetitive manner **mantra**: (in Hinduism and Buddhism) words or sounds which are repeated to help meditation 26 **faqir** (Persian): holy man **shelter**: cover and protection

childlessness. But it is sacred to them for only one day a year. The reason why is open to various interpretations. Some believe that a childless woman had been driven away from her husband's home so that he could marry again. On the day of this second wedding of his she came to hide her shame and grief in Baba Firdaus' grove. Here she had a vision that within nine months of this date she would bear a child; and so it happened. The day of the festival is called *Pati ki Shadi*, or the Husband's Wedding Day. But there are, as I say, various other interpretations, all of them widely differing from and indeed contradicting each other.

Yesterday was the Husband's Wedding Day and I accompanied Inder Lal's mother and her friends to the place of pilgrimage. We went on a bus crammed with women bound for the same destination. Most of them were elderly, and obviously the object of their pilgrimage was, like ours, to have a pleasant outing. Everyone had brought a lot of food which was shared out with many jokes. Some of them had brought barren daughters-in-law, but these remained silent and in the background. Ritu, who had enough children, was left at home.

I have been wanting for some time to see Baba Firdaus' grove, but I didn't get to see much of it yesterday. It was not at all as I had imagined the Nawab's favourite picnic spot! There was a merry little fair going on with rickety roundabouts and a wooden wheel turning round and rows of barrows selling fly-specked food. Devotional songs blared from a loudspeaker attached to a tree. I couldn't even see Baba Firdaus' shrine because there was a tight mass of people wedged in front of it all trying to get near it. We too joined them and pushed in the same direction. By the time we got there, perspiring and struggling within the crowd, it was impossible to have a thought in one's head except to join in whatever was going on. It never became clear to me what this was. There was a priest sitting there receiving offerings. Some of the women – old ones, so they couldn't be invoking the particular blessing of the place – became very devout and shouted out the name of God as if in pain and some of

5 **grief**: deep sorrow 12 **crammed with sb./sth.**: full with sb./sth. 16 **barren**: unfruchtbar, kinderlos 20 **fair**: Jahrmarkt 21 **rickety**: not strong, likely to collapse **roundabout**: merry-go-round, carousel 22 **barrow**: small cart with two wheels **devotional**: religious **blare**: produce sounds loudly and unpleasantly 24 **be wedged in**: eingezwängt/eingekeilt sein 26 **perspire**: sweat

them tried to prostrate themselves though this was difficult on account of there being no room. I didn't know what I was supposed to do but, in any case, just to have got there seemed to be enough.

Our little party found a place under a tree where we all sat in a circle and ate and drank as we had been doing steadily since leaving home. One of the old ladies had a story to tell of a young woman who had been advised an operation on her fallopian tubes but had instead been brought here by her mother-in-law after which conception took place. (Actually, the story ended badly – the woman's husband had had a spell put on him by another woman and this made him drive his wife and her new-born child out of the house). There were more stories, and I liked listening to them, just as I liked sitting here with my friends in the middle of this festive scene. I felt part of it all – absorbed as I had been absorbed by the worshipping crowd packed into the shrine.

My friends turned to me: 'What about you? What did you pray for?' They teased me and laughed. I said they had brought me to the wrong shrine – first they should have taken me to one where not babies but a husband was to be got. More laughter – but really they were being serious (it was a very serious subject), and perhaps I too had thoughts other than usual.

1923

The Husband's Wedding Day was always a very difficult time for Major Minnies. Since Baba Firdaus' shrine lay within the Nawab's state, there was not much that Major Minnies could do except advise. This he did, more and more as the day drew near, nor was he put off by the Nawab laughing at him and saying 'My dear Major, of course, of course, it will be just as you say, why do you worry.' But the Major did worry and not without reason.

In those days Khatm still had a large proportion of Muslim inhabitants (this changed in '47 when they were either killed or emigrated to

1 **prostrate yourself**: lie stretched out on the ground with your face downwards
7 **fallopian tubes**: Eileiter 8 **conception**: Empfängnis 9 **spell** (n): magic words
25 **put sb. off**: jdn. abschrecken

Pakistan). The Nawab himself was a Muslim and so were almost half his subjects. Many of them did not like it when Baba Firdaus' shrine was taken over by Hindu worshippers and always managed to create a disturbance on that day. The disturbance didn't necessarily take place at the shrine itself – two rival groups might clash in the bazaar over some petty issue like a gambling debt, and before long passions rose to that terrible pitch that only religious sentiments could inspire. It did not help that these were days when the summer heat was just getting into its stride (later, as the heat progressed and day followed endless day of it, everyone was too exhausted for strong feeling). So the situation as the day drew near was explosive and the Major said 'Vigilance, vigilance,' and the Nawab good-naturedly laughed at him.

Sure enough, in that first summer of Olivia's, there was rioting in Khatm on the Husband's Wedding Day. Not that Olivia was aware of very much from inside her shuttered bungalow in the Civil Lines: and yet, a certain restlessness penetrated even into her pretty yellow drawing room where she sat playing Schumann on the piano. Everything had to be kept shut tight because there was a dust storm blowing outside. Olivia could not concentrate on Schumann for long. She kept thinking of Douglas: he had tried not to show it, but she knew he had been worried for days. Satipur was the adjoining state to Khatm and communal troubles tended to spread like forest fire. The servants were restless too; they quarrelled a lot with each other, and one of them got drunk and had a fight with another over a woman.

Later in the morning Mrs. Crawford and Mrs. Minnies came to visit her. They had come to reassure her. They told her that there was nothing to worry about in Satipur where all precautions had been taken by Mr. Crawford and Douglas. *Here* there had been proper vigilance: and if only similar attempts could have been made in Khatm as Major Minnies had begged and pleaded with the Nawab – 'But it was the same last year,'

2 **subject**: Untertan 4 **disturbance**: Unruhe 6 **petty**: not very important 8–9 **get into your stride**: (here) begin to be very unpleasant 11 **vigilance**: watchfulness 15 **shuttered** (adj): mit geschlossenen Fensterläden **Civil Lines**: residential area of the British 16 **penetrate into sth.**: get into sth., enter sth. 21 **adjoin**: be next to, be close to 27 **precaution**: measure taken in advance to avoid danger 30 **plead with sb.**: ask sb. desperately (for sth.)

Mrs. Minnies said. 'Arthur had warned him, he had told him over and over … 12 killed and 75 wounded. The whole of the cloth bazaar was gutted – I saw it a week later and it was still smouldering. Arthur says it may be worse this year.'

'It's criminal,' said Mrs. Crawford with deep feeling. 'When he could so easily control it – if he wanted to –'

'The Nawab?' Olivia asked. 'But of course he'd want to!'

'Don't forget he's a Mohammedan too,' they told her.

'Yes but he's not like *that*; not a fanatic. Good heavens.' She laughed at the idea. But their faces remained grim. She urged: 'He's such a modern person. Why, he's just like – almost like one of us in that way. I mean he's not superstitious or bigoted at all. He's so entirely *emancipated*.'

'Do you really think so?' Mrs. Crawford said flatly.

'Oh I'm sure of it. I've heard the way he talked about the suttee, it was just like an English person talking. He was so disgusted. Barbaric, he said.'

'Naturally, he would say that. Suttee is a Hindu custom. It's different when it's anything Mohammedan. Very different then.'

Olivia did not believe them. Of course she could not contradict or even argue with them: that was always the trouble, she never could, she didn't have the right to say anything because they knew everything about India and she nothing. Yet she felt it was *she* who knew the Nawab, not they. To them he was just a person they had to deal with officially, an Indian ruler, but to her he was – yes, a friend. He really was.

She thought she was glad when they left, but in fact she was more uneasy than ever. It was their fault, coming with such tales to frighten her; and talking like that about the Nawab. She paced her drawing room, nervously adjusted her flowers (at this season there was only the heavy almond-scented oleander and jasmine like a drug). Schumann

3 **gutted**: ausgebrannt **smoulder**: burn slowly without a flame 10 **urge (sb.)**: try hard to persuade sb. 12 **superstitious**: abergläubisch **bigoted** (adj): bigott; fanatisch 14 **flatly** (adv): unemotionally 28 **pace sth.**: walk through sth. 29 **adjust sth.**: rearrange sth. 30 **almond-scented oleander**: nach Mandeln duftender Oleander

was impossible, she shut the piano. She began to write to Marcia, but Marcia was in Paris and it was impossible to *explain* anything from here to there.

She heard the sound of a car outside. The Nawab! Her heart beat – she didn't know with what strong emotion. She opened the door leading to the verandah and found the servants clustered there with their heads close together. When they saw her, they got quickly to their feet. The dust got instantly into her eyes, nostrils, between her teeth; it blew in gusts into the room. 'It's me!' cried a voice from the car. It was not the Nawab but Harry.

He hurried in with her and the door was quickly shut again. But already, even from that one moment, the desert dust lay in a thick layer on her piano and the yellow silk of her armchairs.

'Are you alone?' she asked.

He nodded. He seemed very glad to have arrived and sat with his head back and his eyes shut.

'I *had* to come,' he said; 'It was too –'

He stopped as two servants came in. They flapped vigorously at the furniture to get the dust out. Harry and Olivia were silent, waiting for the servants to go out again. By the time they did, Harry seemed to have changed his mind about what he was going to say; now he tried to sound flippant: 'I was parched for the oasis.'

'What's happening in Khatm?' He didn't answer but shut his eyes again. She said 'I hear there are some sort of – riots?' She insisted: 'What's it all about? Tell me. No you must.'

After a pause he said, quite fretfully: 'How should I know? After all, I live in the Palace and nothing like that happens there, does it.'

'Nothing like what?'

'How should I know,' he repeated. 'I stayed in my room all day yesterday and this morning. What else can you do in this hideous ter-

8 **nostril**: Nasenloch 9 **gust**: sudden strong rush of wind 12 **layer**: thickness of a substance that lies on top of sth. 18 **flap**: move or swing your hands up and down **vigorous**: energetic, forceful 22 **flippant**: schnodderig **parched** (adj): dried out and very thirsty 26 **fretful**: wehleidig, kläglich 30 **hideous** (adj): horrible

rible heat. Have you looked outside? Have you *seen* what it's like? Once these dust storms start, they go on for ever. No wonder everyone goes mad.' He was silent for a while as if afraid of saying too much: but next moment he said more, talking rather fast: 'I was going mad myself. Locked up in that room and thinking of what was going on. Don't ask me what! I wouldn't know. It was the same last year, and the year before. But this year, thank goodness, I had somewhere to go to. When I asked him for a car to bring me here, he said 'Certainly, certainly, my dear fellow.' Even though he was so ... preoccupied, he still had time to make arrangements for me. He told the chauffeur which way to go so we wouldn't run into anything. And we didn't. Just shouting from the bazaar area but that could have been anything really, couldn't it. When I asked him would it be safe for me in the car, he said 'What, in *my* car?' He thought that was a great joke. Olivia, do play something. Anything.'

She sat at the piano and, as she began to play more Schumann, he said 'Lovely' like a man being given a cool drink. But after a time she sensed that he wasn't listening any more. She let her hands slide from the keys into her lap. He didn't even notice that she had stopped.

'Coming to think of it,' he said, 'it's almost worse *inside* the Palace. Because of all those people coming and going, such low-class ruffians, the sort you'd never see in the Palace otherwise. But now they're walking in and out as if they owned the place, and straight into his presence as if that's their right. And he's so eager to see them and hear what they have to say, and if he likes it he embraces them like they were his brothers. You should see them, what types ... Is there anyone out there?'

'I think the servants.'

She peered through the glass and, sure enough, there they were squatting in a cluster as before. Instinctively aware of being watched, they got up and dispersed. She came back and sat quite close to Harry, so that he could talk in a lower voice:

17 **sense sth.**: become aware of sth. 18 **key**: Klaviertaste **lap**: Schoß 20 **ruffian** (old-fashioned): Rüpel 23 **eager** ['iːgə]: full of enthusiasm 24 **embrace sb.**: hold sb. in your arms 27 **peer**: look 28 **squat**: kauern 29 **disperse**: go into different directions

'And *he's* strange. I never see him like that except during these days. He is terribly excited and doesn't seem able to stay still, waiting all the time: I don't know for what. His eyes burn, they really do. And anything will set him off laughing. He rocks on his heels as he laughs.' Harry shut his eyes: 'He looks devastatingly handsome.' He didn't say this with pleasure but as if it exhausted him.

Although Douglas came home very late that night, Harry was still there. If Douglas did not like Harry – and Olivia knew he didn't – he gave no sign of it but, on the contrary, seemed glad that he had come. He wouldn't hear of Harry going back that night but ordered the Nawab's chauffeur to take the car to Khatm without him. Harry seemed relieved: also to sit down to dinner with the two of them at their table which Olivia always made so pretty with candles and flowers.

Harry stayed that night and the next day and the day after that. He and Olivia were very good company for each other. They didn't care about the dust storm blowing outside but just locked all the doors and windows and curled up in the yellow armchairs. Olivia played excerpts from *I Pagliacci* and Harry sang in an exaggerated voice, his hand on his heart. They didn't notice Mrs. Crawford come in, and when they did, she wouldn't let them stop but joined in herself with a fine contralto. 'What fun,' she said and laughed like the good sport she was.

She had come to talk about Simla. She said she didn't want to nag Olivia, but she felt that perhaps Olivia didn't quite understand – here she turned to Harry as if asking him for his support.

He gave it: 'You shouldn't be here through the summer, Olivia. It's unbearable.'

'If *you* can bear it -'

'Who said I could.'

But then he was embarrassed like a person who has shown more feeling than is decent. He tried to laugh it off: 'Of course a thousand

4 **rock** (v): schaukeln 5 **devastating** (adj; infml): impressive, irresistable
17 **curl up**: sit with your back curved and legs drawn up close to the body
20 **contralto**: Altstimme 21 **be a good sport**: ein feiner Kerl sein 22 **nag sb.**: bother sb. continually

plans are afoot to leave immediately for Mussoorie. We've even packed and unpacked a couple of times.' He laughed again though with a nervous tremor: 'Exactly the same happened last year, and the year before ... In the end we never did go. The Begum doesn't like it there so she keeps putting it off. Either she's not feeling well or the stars are not right for a journey or an owl hooted at the wrong time – it's always something or other and always at the last moment when we're all packed and ready. I've got used to it now, like everyone else. Once we really did leave, in my first year. He has a marvellous house up there – it's a Swiss chalet with a dash of Gothic cathedral, very impressive indeed. So is the view. You can look right across to – what's the name of that mountain where Siva is supposed to sit amid the eternal snows? Not that I got much time to enjoy it. A dead bat was found in – of all places – the Begum's bedroom and that of course is a terrible omen so we had to pack up and come home immediately and as soon as we got here ceremonies had to be performed for about three weeks without stop.' Suddenly he turned to Mrs. Crawford and spoke in a rush 'Mother keeps writing for me to come – she's not well and I am worried about her, she lives alone in a flat you see and it's been three years now.'

'That *is* long,' said Mrs. Crawford.

'It was only supposed to be six months, but whenever I mention about going home – because of Mother, mostly – he doesn't like it. He hates people leaving him.' Then he said: 'It's because he gets terribly involved with his friends, that's the reason because he's so ... *affectionate*. Warm-hearted. He has a warm heart.' He looked down at the floor.

After a while Mrs. Crawford said in her bright practical voice: 'Do you know the Ross-Milbanks? He's been the D.C. over at Cawnpore. They're going on home leave now – driving down to Bombay to get the P. & O. – I think it's the S.S. *Maloja* – on the 4th. They're spending a couple of nights with us on their way. We *are* looking forward to it. That

1 **afoot**: being prepared or planned **Mussoorie**: mountain town in north India
3 **tremor**: slight shaking 6 **hoot**: cry 10 **a dash of sth.**: ein Schuss von etwas
12 **Siva = Shiva** (cf. p. ÜÜ): this is a reference to Mount Kailish 27 **D.C.**: District Commisioner 29 **P. & O. = Peninsular and Oriental**: shipping line that connected Britain and many of the colonies **S.S.** (abbr): steamship

really is one of the great pleasures of India, isn't it, people from all over the country dropping in on you.'

He said: 'But those P. & O.s, aren't they always booked up, aren't they completely? Months ahead?'

'Oh a single berth,' Mrs. Crawford said. 'And one could always send a cable to the Gibbons in Bombay ...'

'Really?' Harry said – so full of glad hope that she smiled: 'Really and truly,' she promised him.

That night, when they were in bed together under their mosquito net, Olivia asked Douglas: 'But if he's the Nawab's guest?'

'So what.'

'But the Nawab paid his fare. And has been keeping him in the lap of luxury, hasn't he, all this time. I can't see how he can just ... run out on him.' She added: 'With Mrs. Crawford's friends.'

'Darling, he *wants* to go.'

'Sometimes he does. Sometimes he doesn't.'

'That's too subtle for me. Anyway, he ought to want to.'

'Are you tired of having him here?'

'On the contrary. I'm glad he is here. Better than being over there.'

'But the Nawab has been so kind to him! Terribly kind!'

'Tomorrow I'll send someone over for his luggage.'

'Douglas, are you *sure*, darling.'

But on the next day – a Sunday – the Nawab came himself. Olivia and Douglas had been to church, and when they got home, the Nawab's Rolls was outside the house; and the Nawab himself in the drawing room with Harry who was still in his pyjamas and dressing-gown. They looked as if they had already had a long and intimate conversation together.

When the Nawab said he had come to take Harry home, Douglas stiffened. The Nawab became more cordial, he said thank you very much for keeping him; and added, 'Now all is quiet at Khatm, he need not be afraid any longer.' He smiled at Harry who smiled back, bashfully.

2 **drop in on sb.** (infml): pay a visit to sb. 6 **cable**: telegram 26 **dressing-gown**: Morgenmantel 29 **stiffen**: become less friendly or anxious **cordial**: friendly 31 **bashful**: verlegen, schüchtern

Douglas clenched his jaws; there was a little muscle working in them. The Nawab said 'You have probably heard that we had a little trouble.'

Douglas stared straight ahead of him. He and the Nawab were both standing. They were the same height and almost the same build. Olivia and Harry, seated on sofas, looked up at them.

'It happens every year,' the Nawab said. 'It is nothing much. They get hot – they become cool again. It is like the weather in its season.'

'We saw your casualty lists,' Douglas said in a strangled voice.

'But why are you standing!' Olivia cried. No one heard her.

'It happens every year,' the Nawab repeated. 'There is nothing to be done.'

Douglas turned aside his face. He had to be silent – the Nawab was an independent ruler, and the only person who could speak to him was Major Minnies. But Douglas' silence was eloquent of all he could have said, and of his thoughts.

The Nawab turned to Harry: 'Get dressed. We are going.'

Harry got up at once but, before he could leave the room, Douglas said 'I believe the Ross-Milbanks are expected tomorrow afternoon.'

Harry stopped by the door; the Nawab asked him in a casual way 'Who are they? Are they your friends?'

'They leave on Thursday,' Douglas said.

'Oh for Bombay?' the Nawab said. 'Yes Harry has told me about that, but it is cancelled now. My dear fellow, please get dressed, you don't expect me to take you home in this state I hope.' He turned and smiled at Olivia.

Douglas told Harry: 'Mr. Crawford has heard from Bombay. It's all right about the berth.'

The Nawab now sat down in an armchair. He leaned back, crossed his legs. He told Douglas: 'Harry and I have talked about it. It has all been a misunderstanding. I shall apologise to Mr. and Mrs. Crawford and thank them for their kind efforts on behalf of my guest. I shall also thank,' he added generously, 'Mr. and Mrs. Ross-Milbank.'

1 **clench sth.**: press sth. together 8 **casualty**: person killed or wounded in an accident or in battle 14 **eloquent**: (here) showing something very strongly without words 31 **on behalf of sb.**: for sb., in the interests of sb.

Douglas made no bones about addressing only Harry: 'You wanted to go. Your mother's ill.'

The Nawab said: 'We have to be very thankful: Mother is better, she has recovered her health ... And now we are very much looking forward to her visit. My Mother has written to invite her – her letter is in Urdu, written in her own hand, and I myself have made a translation into English and also added: "You now have not one son but two and both your sons are eager for your visit." He leaned back further in his chair and crossed his legs the other way, pleased with the correct way in which everything had been done.

Harry took a deep breath and told Douglas: 'Thanks awfully for having me. It's true, you know – I do want to go back to the Palace. We talked it over before you came, as he told you. I do want to.'

'You don't have to,' Douglas told him from the other side of the room.

'I want to,' Harry said.

The Nawab burst out laughing: 'But don't you see, Mr. and Mrs. Rivers, he is like a child that doesn't know what it wants! We others have to decide everything for him. Just see,' he said, 'it is I who have to tell him get dressed, Harry, this is not the way to stand before a lady, go and get ready, comb your hair nicely.' He gave a quick playful stroke at Harry's head and they both smiled as if it were an old joke between them. 'Go,' said the Nawab with tender strictness, and when Harry had gone, he turned to the other two: 'Did you know,' he asked them very seriously, 'that Harry is a very selfish person?' Then he sighed and said 'But what can I do – I have grown fond of him, he has his place here.' He placed his hand on his heart.

Olivia looked quickly at Douglas. She was sorry to see that he remained as before. For herself, she had no doubt at all that the Nawab was utterly sincere: so that she was even somewhat envious of Harry for having inspired such a depth of love and friendship.

* * * *

1 **make no bones about (doing) sth.**: feel no doubt or shame about (doing) sth.
30 **utterly** (adv): completely

25 April. Chid and I have now both merged into the landscape: we are part of the town, part of people's lives here, and have been completely accepted. The town is used to accepting and merging all sorts of different elements – for instance, the grand old tombs of Mohammedan royalty on the one hand and the little grey suttee stones on the other. There are also the town's cripples, idiots, and resident beggars. They move around the streets and, whenever anything of interest is going on, they rush up and form part of the crowd. Like everyone else, I have got used to them now – as they have to me – but I must admit that in the beginning I couldn't help shrinking a bit. Some diseases, even when cured, leave people so unsightly that for the rest of their lives they have to move among their fellows as living examples of all the terrible things that can happen to a man. One of the beggars is a cured leper – a burnt-out case whose nose, fingers, and toes have dropped off; he lives in a hut some distance out of town but is allowed to come in and beg, provided he keeps at a proper distance. Then there is an old man who I think has St. Vitus's dance – his body is twisted around a long pole he carries and he hops along twitching and jigging like a puppet. It is not only the poor and the beggars who have afflictions. One of the most prosperous shop-keepers in town who is also a moneylender suffers from elephantiasis and can be seen sitting in his shop with his scrotum, swollen literally to the size of a football, resting on a special little cushion in front of him.

Dust storms have started blowing all day, all night. Hot winds whistle columns of dust out of the desert into the town; the air is choked with dust and so are all one's senses. Leaves that were once green are now ashen, and they toss around as in a dervish dance. Everyone is restless, irritable, on the edge of something. It is impossible to sit, stand, lie, every position is uncomfortable; and one's mind too is in turmoil.

1 **merge into sth.**: verschmelzen, mit etwas fusionieren 6 **resident beggar**: beggar who lives permanently in a town 11 **unsightly**: unpleasant to look at 13 **leper**: Leprakranker 16–17 **St. Vitus's dance**: movement disorder 17 **pole**: Stab, Stange 18 **twitch**: make quick short sudden uncontrollable movements **jig**: move up and down with quick short movements 19 **affliction**: pain, suffering 20 **elephantiasis**: swelling caused by parasites or worms in the body 21 **scrotum**: Hodensack 26 **dervish dance**: spiritual Muslim dance in which the dances whirl round and round 28 **turmoil**: Aufruhr, Durcheinander

Chid doesn't seem to be affected by the weather. He sits for hours together in the lotus pose, his lips moving on his mantra and his fingers on his beads: and this goes on and on and seems somehow so *mindless* that it drives me crazy. It is as if all reason and common sense are being drained out of the air. Every now and again he gets those monstrous erections of his and I have to fight him off (quite apart from anything else, it's just too *hot*). He is also dirty – bathing is one Hindu ritual he doesn't practise – and since he doesn't believe in possessions for himself he thinks other people shouldn't have any either. I have had to start hiding my money, but he is quite clever at finding it.

Today I got so exasperated with him, I threw him out. I just bundled up his belongings and flung them down the stairs. His brass mug bounced down the steps and was caught at the bottom of them by Ritu who had chosen that moment to come and visit me. Chid gathered up his things and, following her back upstairs, laid them out again in their former place.

'You can't stay,' I told him.

But I couldn't say any more because of Ritu. She was in a strange state. She sat in a corner with her knees drawn up and didn't say one word. She looked frightened – she was like a little wild animal that had rushed in for protection. Although I did not feel in a fit condition to protect anyone, I tried to pull myself together and speak to her in a calm way. I don't think she even heard. Her eyes continued to dart around the room, but she seemed not to see anything either. Chid sat cross-legged in the corner opposite the one where she crouched. His eyes were shut, his beads slipped through his fingers, he chanted. He made me mad.

'You can't stay!' I shouted at him.

But his chanting had transported him elsewhere – perhaps into wider, cooler, brighter, more beautiful regions. He swayed lightly, his beads went on slipping, his lips moved; he was blissful. Ritu began to scream the way she had done that night. Chid opened his eyes, looked at her, then shut then; again and went on chanting. They both got louder

2 **lotus pose**: way of sitting with your legs crossed in order to meditate
5 **drain**: flow out completely 11 **exasperasted** (adj): annoyed 12 **brass mug**: Becher aus Blech 25 **crouch**: kauern 29 **sway**: swing slowly from side to side
30 **blissful**: extremely happy

– like communicants of two rival sects, each trying to prove the superiority of his faith by outshouting the other.

30 April. As the heat and dust storms continue, Ritu's condition has become worse. She has now to be kept locked up inside the room and sometimes terrible sounds come from out of there. The other people living around the courtyard seem to be quite used to them and continue to move around their business undisturbed. Chid is also quite undisturbed. He says he has been in India long enough to have got used to everything. But I can't get used to these screams. I kept telling Chid 'But she ought to have treatment.'

One day he said 'She's going to have treatment today.'

'What sort?' I asked.

'One of their people is coming to do it.'

That day the screams broke out again, but in an entirely different way. Now they were bloodcurdling as of an animal in intense physical pain. Even the neighbours in the courtyard stopped to listen. Chid remained calm: 'It's her treatment,' he said. He went on to explain that she might be possessed by an evil spirit which had to be driven out by applying a red-hot iron to various parts of her body, such as her arms or the soles of her feet.

Next day I decided to speak to Inder Lal about psychiatric treatment. I waited for him outside his office, and as we walked home together, I tried to explain to him what it was. I said 'It's a sort of science of the mind,' which pleased him and made him attentive. He associates science with progress and everything else modern and up-to-date that he is eager to learn about; when anyone speaks about such things, his face takes on an expression of wistful desire.

But when I mentioned the 'treatment' to which Ritu had been subjected, he changed again. He became both melancholy and embarrassed; he said 'I don't believe in these things.'

'But you had it done.'

1 **communicant**: person who receives communion in a Christian church service; (here) followers, believers 15 **bloodcurdling** (adj): Grauen erregend 27 **wistful**: wehmütig, schwermütig

'Mother wanted it.'

He went on to defend both himself and her. He said all her friends had advised it; they had cited many cases where it had effected a cure. At first his mother had also been reluctant, but then she said 'Why not try,' and in the end he too said 'why not,' for they had tried everything else but had not succeeded in relieving Ritu's suffering.

Just then one of his colleagues passed us and greeted me very politely. They have all got used to me now and often take the opportunity of having conversation in English. Of course I greeted him back again, but Inder Lal did not care for this exchange. He frowned, and when the man was out of earshot, said 'Why does he pretend to be so friendly.'

'He *is* friendly.'

Inder Lal's frown deepened. He wouldn't talk for a while but brooded in his thoughts.

'But what's he done?' I asked.

Inder Lal implored me not to speak so loudly. He looked over his shoulder which made me laugh.

'You don't know,' he said then. His whole face had closed up with fear and suspicion. 'You don't know what people are like or what is in their hearts even when they are smiling with friendly faces. Again yesterday there was an anonymous letter,' he said, lowering his voice.

'Against you?'

He would not say. He walked beside me in brooding silence. I hate to see him like that, with all the brightness of his nature obscured by dark suspicions.

2 May. Where I advised psychiatry, Maji – the holy woman and friend – has advised pilgrimage. Inder Lal's mother and Ritu are to leave in a few days time: best of all, Chid is going with them! Maji has persuaded him to do so; I almost feel she did it for my sake – not that I ever complained to her about Chid, but she seems to know most things by herself.

3 **cite sth.**: mention sth. as an example 11 **out of earshot**: where one cannot be heard 13 **brood**: think about sth. for a long time 16 **implore sb.**: beg sb. for sth. in a serious way 24 **obscure sth.**: hide sth.

She told me yesterday when I had gone to pay her a visit. At first we sat inside her hut, but it got so stifling in there that we crawled out again, even though the hot wind was still blowing. The dust swirled around the royal tombs and sat in a pall over the lake. Chid was with us too. He often visits Maji – he says he derives great benefit from her presence. They make a strange couple together. Maji is a very earthy-looking peasant woman; she is quite fat and always jolly. Whenever she looks at Chid, she gives a shout of laughter; 'Good boy!' she cries – in English, perhaps her only two words in it. He does look like a good boy when he is with her – sitting very straight in his meditation pose and a spiritual if rather strained look on his face.

Maji explained to me about pilgrimages. She said 'If someone is very unhappy and disturbed in their minds, or if they have some great wish to be fulfilled, or a terrible longing inside them, then they go. It is a long long journey, high up in the Himalayas. Very beautiful and holy. When she comes back,' she said about Ritu, 'her heart will be at ease.'

She patted my knee – she likes touching people – and asked 'Would you like to go?' She pointed at Chid: 'Oh how he will love it, this good boy!' She laughed loudly, then took his cheeks between her hands and squeezed them lovingly. 'Are you going?' I asked him, but he shut his eyes and murmured '*Om*.'

Maji said 'All sorts of people go from all over India. They travel for weeks and months away from their homes in order to reach there. On the way they stop at temple rest-houses, and when they come to a river they bathe in it. They travel very slowly and if they like a place they stay there for a while and take their rest. At last they reach the mountains and begin to climb up. What shall I say of that place, those mountains!' cried Maji. 'Yes it is climbing up into heaven. There is cool air and breezes, clouds, birds, and trees. Then there is only snow, everything is white and the sun also is shining white. Having bathed in the icy stream,

2 **stifling** ['staɪflɪŋ] (adj.): make sb. unable to breathe because of lack of fresh air
4 **pall** (n): dark or heavy covering 5 **derive sth. from sb./sth.**: get sth. from sb./sth. 7 **jolly**: happy, cheerful 11 **strained** (adj): uncomfortable, not relaxed
16 **at ease**: relaxed and peaceful 21 **Om**: (in Hinduism and Buddhism) religious word (mantra) used in meditation

they draw near the cave at last. Many faint and fall down with joy and none can restrain himself, they call out the Name at the top of their voices. *Jai Shiva Shankar*!' she called out at the top of her voice.

'*Jai Shiva Shankar*!' Chid echoed at the top of his.

'Good boy! Good boy!' she cried and encouraged him to repeat it in chorus with her. It really sounded as if it were echoing through those snowy mountains she had mentioned, and I must say, sitting here in the dust storm under the yellow sky, I too would have liked to be up there.

1923

Mrs. Crawford and Mrs. Minnies had left for Simla. Although Douglas had done his best to persuade Olivia to accompany them, now that she had decided to stay he was very grateful and happy. They spent lovely evenings and nights together. Olivia tried to be lively and gay for him. She understood that, once Douglas was home, he just wanted to *be* home, with her, in their tasteful English bungalow, leaving outside all the heat and problems he had to contend with the whole day long. So she never touched on any subject that might cast even the faintest shadow on him – like, for instance, that of the Nawab – but chattered to him about everything she could think of that had nothing to do with India. Douglas loved her more than ever at this time, if that were possible. Inarticulate by nature, sometimes he reached such a pitch of high emotion that he felt he had to express it: but his feelings were always too strong for him and made him stutter.

Harry usually came quite early in the mornings, just after Douglas had left, and always in one of the Nawab's cars. He and Olivia sat in the car and drove to Khatm. Although the way was so hot and dusty, the landscape utterly flat and monotonous, Olivia learned to like these morning drives. Sometimes she glanced out of the window and then she thought well it was not so bad really – she could even see how one could learn to like it (in fact, she *was* learning): the vast distances, the

2 **restrain yourself**: keep yourself under control 3 **Jai Shiva Shankar** (Hindi): Hail to thee, Great God Shiva 16 **contend with sb./sth.**: mit jdm./etwas zu tun haben 17 **cast sth.**: throw sth. (esp. a light or shadow) **faint**: very small, hardly noticeable

vast sky, the dust and sun and occasional broken fort or mosque or cluster of tombs. It was so different from what one knew that it was like being not in a different part of this world but in another world altogether, in another reality.

They usually spent the day in the large drawing-room in the Palace. This was overlooked by a curtained gallery from which the ladies sometimes watched them; but Olivia never looked up. Besides the Nawab and Harry, there were the usual young men lying around in graceful attitudes. They drank, smoked, played cards, and were perfectly content to go on doing that till the Nawab told them to do something else.

One day the Nawab said 'Olivia' – this was what he called her now – 'Olivia, you play the piano so beautifully but you have never played mine.'

'Where is it?'

She looked around the drawing-room. It was a long cool marble room furnished very sparsely with just a few pieces of European furniture between the pillars. There were carved sofas with brocade upholstery and a few little carved tables and a cocktail cabinet specially made for the Nawab out of an elephant's foot: but no piano.

The Nawab laughed: 'Come, I will show you.'

He did not invite anyone else to follow him. He led her through various suites and passages. She never could find her way around the Palace: not that it was very large but it was intricate, and there were certain areas where she had never been and had no idea what went on there, if anything. He took her into an underground chamber which seemed to be a kind of store room. And what stores! There was an immense amount of camera equipment which, though already rusting, did not seem ever to have been used; some of it was still in its original packing. The same had happened to some modern sanitary equipment and an assortment of games such as a pinball machine, a croquet set, a miniature shooting gallery, meccano sets, and equipment for a hockey

2 **cluster**: group 17 **pillar**: Säule 18 **upholstery**: Polsterung, Bezug
23 **intricate**: composed of many small parts put together in a complex way
30 **assortment**: Mischung, Auswahl 31 **meccano set**: toy construction set of small metal or plastic pieces used to build machines, etc.

team. All of these things appeared to have been ordered from Europe but had taken too long to arrive for interest in them to be sustained. There was not one piano but two: a grand and an upright.

As the Nawab touched the baize cloth covering the grand piano, a small animal – it looked like a squirrel – came scurrying out and ran for its life. The Nawab did not seem surprised: 'Do you like my pianos?' he asked Olivia; and added apologetically 'There is no one to play them.'

The keys were swollen and stuck, and when Olivia tried to play some of them, all she could get was a shrill jangle. 'What a shame,' she said with feeling.

'Yes,' he said. 'Yes you are right.' He too was suddenly sad. He sank down on to an unopened packing-case. After a heavy silence he said 'They were ordered for my wife.'

Olivia tried again but the sounds produced were too heartbreaking.

'Can they be mended?' he asked.

'If you can get a good tuner.'

'Certainly. I will send for it immediately.'

'It's a person,' Olivia said. 'I've been desperately wanting someone but Douglas says he has to come all the way from Bombay.'

'Why didn't you tell me? Such things you must tell me. There is so little I can do to serve my friends. Did you know I was married?'

'I've heard,' Olivia murmured.

He leaned forward: 'What have you heard?' His eyes scanned her face which she kept lowered and, she hoped, expressionless. Nevertheless he seemed to have read something into it.

He said 'You will hear many things about me. There are many people to give bad report. Whatever I do – there are always those who will say one thing when it is another. You know Murad?' Olivia knew him to be one of the young men who were always there, but it was difficult to distinguish one from another. 'He is a spy,' the Nawab said. 'Oh I know it and he knows I know it, we understand each other. And he is not the only one. There are others, among the servants and everyone.' His eyes

2 **sustain sb./sth.**: keep sb. / sth. alive 3 **grand (piano)**: Flügel **upright (piano)**: Klavier 4 **baize**: grüner Wollstoff 5 **scurry**: run with short quick steps 9 **jangle**: harsh noise 15 **mend sth.**: etwas reparieren, ausbessern 16 **tuner**: person who adjusts a musical instrument to the correct sound

as they rested on Olivia were veiled with dark thoughts. If he suspected her too – and he probably did – she knew no way to defend herself.

But he reverted to the pianos: 'If I have them repaired and brought upstairs, you will come and play for me, Olivia? It will make me so very happy. Sandy had been learning the sitar but she got tired of it so I sent for the pianos. By the time they arrived she had gone away. Please play.'

'But it sounds so awful.'

'For my sake.'

He stood behind her while she tried to play a Bach Prelude. It was murder, but he nodded solemnly as if he liked it. He bent over her closely.

'I wish Sandy could have learned to play like you. I miss her very much. She was supposed to be in purdah upstairs but she often hid from everyone to come and be with me. You see, she was a modern girl, she went to school in Switzerland and all the rest. She was not like our other Indian ladies but – yes, like you, Olivia. She was like you. Also beautiful like you.'

Olivia had now got to some intricate trills. She played them as well as she could, but the sounds that came out were tuneless and eerie. In any case, he seemed to have lost interest in the piano music. He straightened up with a sigh and, though she was still in the middle of her piece, turned to go out. She had to break off and follow him as she did not think she could find the way back by herself.

It was about this time – the time of her growing friendship with the Nawab – that she and Douglas began to speak seriously about having children. They were both very keen on it. Olivia felt that someone as handsome, as perfect as Douglas should be procreated many times over! She teased him about it – she said he had only married her so as to people the world with a whole lot of Douglases. Not at all, he said; it was Olivias he wanted – as many of them as possible.

3 **revert to sth.**: return to sth. (e.g. an earlier topic) 9 **prelude**: Präludium
10 **solemn**: sincere, serious 13 **purdah**: the practise in some Islamic countries of keeping women seperate from men behind curtains so that they could not be seen
18 **trill**: Triller 27 **procreate sb.** (fml): reproduce sb. sexually

'Oh but I'm unique, don't you know.'

'Of course you are. Absolutely,' he agreed with enthusiasm. He bent down to kiss her naked shoulder. They were getting dressed for dinner – they were expecting the two grass-widowers, Mr. Crawford and Major Minnies – and Olivia sat at her dressing-table in her cream silk slip, liberally dousing herself with lavender water.

They went on speaking about their sons. Olivia liked to think of these tall pro-consuls – one in the army, one a civilian like Douglas, perhaps a political? All of them in India of course – but she did have one doubt: 'Supposing things change – I mean, what with Mr. Gandhi and these people' – but she trailed off, seeing Douglas smile behind her in the mirror. *He* had no doubts at all, he said 'They'll need us a while longer,' with easy amused assurance. He was in shirtsleeves and braces and raised his chin to tie his black bow tie.

'And what about Olivia?' she asked, set at ease about her sons.

Douglas had no doubts about her either – she was going to marry into a family just like her own, to someone like her brothers, and become like –

'Mrs. Crawford?'

Douglas smiled again: 'No like Olivia – I'll settle for nothing less.'

'Oh Olivia's no good,' she said with sudden deep conviction, even a kind of self-disgust. He didn't notice the change of tone – he laughed and said 'Good enough for me.' But when he tried to kiss her shoulder again, she got up quickly and began to slip her dress over her head. 'They'll be here soon,' she said. 'You'd better go.'

She had had a table carried out into the garden and arranged it very decoratively. The gentlemen appreciated all her feminine touches. Their mood became relaxed, even though it was a hot night and they of course in dinner jackets. They spoke of the absent ladies. The news from Simla was good: Honeysuckle Cottage had come up to expectations and the

4 **grass-widower**: man whose wife is absent for a period of time 6 **douse yourself**: sich übergießen 8 **pro-consul**: deputy consul (position in the administration in India) 11 **trail off**: become gradually quieter and then stop speaking
13 **shirtsleeves**: short sleeved shirt **braces** (pl): Hosenträger 14 **bow tie**: Fliege
20 **settle for sth.**: accept sth. that is seen as not quite satisfactory 21 **conviction**: Überzeugung 22 **self-disgust**: Abscheu

weather was so cool that they had even lit a fire one night! Not so much because they needed it (Mrs. Crawford had confessed) but because it was such a treat to see it roaring in the big cosy fireplace.

Major Minnies said 'That's one treat we can very well do without, down here.' He mopped his face which was glistening with perspiration; but nevertheless he was smiling, contented. He raised his glass to Olivia. 'We owe a toast to our hostess who has remained with us in our ordeal of fire.'

'Yes indeed' and 'Rather' said Mr. Crawford, also raising his glass to her. So did Douglas. Olivia saw their three faces beaming at her. 'Oh nonsense,' she murmured and looked down at her hand lying on the tablecloth. She felt enveloped in their admiration and gratitude. They all drank the cool wine. The moon had risen behind the house, making it look like a silhouetted stage-set; servants came out of it in procession, bearing the next course. The garden was full of the summer smells of jasmine and Queen of the Night. At its furthest end, huddled against the wall, were the servants quarters exuding muffled but incessant sounds.

'What about you, Minnies?' Mr. Crawford asked. 'When will you be deserting us for cooler climes?' When Major Minnies shook his head, he said sympathetically 'Our Friend is still playing up, is he. Hard luck.'

'Oh I'm used to it,' said Major Minnies good naturedly. 'Except I wish it hadn't all come up at this particular season. Poor Mary. We haven't had a Simla holiday together since, let me see, yes it was in '19. Two years ago of course we had the Cabobpur affair and this year –' He made a gesture, assuming they all knew what it was *this* year. And of course they did, only too well; except Olivia who hazarded 'Is it still,' in a nervous voice, 'that awful Husband's Wedding Day thing?'

'No dear lady,' said Major Minnies, 'Husband's Wedding Day has come and gone. We got off relatively cheaply this time: only 6 killed and

5 **mop your face**: wipe your face 6 **contented**: satisfied 7 **ordeal**: difficult, painful situation 14 **stage-set**: Bühnenbild 16 **Queen of the Night**: type of cactus whose flowers open after sunset 17 **exude sth.**: etwas verströmen, verbreiten **muffled** (adj): not heard clearly **incessant**: never stopping
19 **climes** (old-fashioned): area with a special climate 26 **hazard sth**: etwas (z. B. eine Bemerkung) wagen, riskieren

43 wounded. Let us be thankful for small mercies amen – and yes let us also pray that we shall extricate ourselves from the dacoit affair without too much of a bust-up ... At present,' he said, 'I wouldn't like to be in that boy's shoes.'

'Which boy's shoes?' said Olivia. She called to Douglas across the table – 'Darling, what are you doing, do tell them to get the other bottle.' 'Sorry sorry sorry,' said Douglas, tearing himself away from the conversation to motion to the head bearer.

'Our Friend's', said Major Minnies.

'They're taking a grave view, are they,' said Mr. Crawford.

'Very much so. I've been trying to use moderate language in my reports but, dash it all, it's not easy to be moderate when you have to stand by and see a recognised ruler turning himself into a dacoit chief.'

'A dacoit chief!' cried Olivia. It came out really startled and she shot a quick look at Douglas: but he hadn't noticed, he was too indignant himself and all his attention was on Major Minnies.

'Of course we all know the fellow's bankrupt,' Major Minnies said, 'that's nothing new. What is new is that, having bled his unfortunate subjects white by means of more or less legitimate extortion, he is now taking to cruder methods. In fact, not to put too fine a point on it, to outright robbery.'

He was silent in order to collect himself. He was genuinely outraged. The others too were silent. A bird woke up in a tree and gave a shriek. Perhaps it had been dreaming of a snake, or perhaps there really *was* a snake.

'I envy you chaps in the districts,' Major Minnies said. 'Dealing only with banyas and peasants who can be – well – what shall I say – understandable. Containable.'

1 **be thankful for small mercies**: schon für Weniges dankbar sein 2 **extricate yourself from sth.**: free yourself from sth. 3 **bust-up**: very angry disagreement
8 **motion to sb.**: give sb. a signal to do sth. 10 **grave**: serious 12 **dash it all** (old-fashioned): expression of annoyance or anger 15 **indignant**: empört
18–19 **bleed (bled – bled) sb. white**: take away all sb.'s money from them (through taxes, etc.) 19 **extortion**: Erpressung 20 **crude**: primitive **not to put too fine a point on it**: um nicht um den heißen Brei herumzureden 21 **outright**: open and obvious 22 **outraged** (adj): very shocked and angry 27 **banya** (Hindi): Indian trader 28 **containable**: able to be controlled

'Pretty decent sorts some of them,' confirmed Mr. Crawford.

'Quite,' said the Major. Again he had to master some strong emotion before he could continue: 'At one time I was supposed to be advising the Maharaja of Dhung. It was when he was building his new palace – perhaps you've seen it? At least you must have heard of it, it caused a great hullaballoo. The latter-day Versailles it was to be. In fact, it turned into a most hideous hotch-potch with a pepper pot roof on Doric columns, but that's not the point. The point is that, at the time HH was a-building, the monsoons failed twice in succession and Dhung along with all the surrounding districts was under threat of famine. HH was too busy to notice, or to listen to any of us. I had the heck of a time even getting to see him, he was always so busy with the people he had imported from Europe. There was an architect, and a decorator, and a *tailor* if you please, from Vienna (for the curtains), also a champion swimmer – female – to inaugurate the underground swimming pool … When I managed at last to pour my tale of woe into his luckless ear, he called me an old fuddy-duddy. He loved these expressions – he'd been at Eton. 'You're an old fuddy-duddy, Major,' he said. And then he grew very serious and drew himself up to his full height which was almost five feet and he said 'The trouble with you, my dear fellow, I'm sorry to tell you is you have no vision. No vision at all.' Unfortunately it turned out that I did have some – at any rate more than he – because there *was* a famine. You remember '12.'

'Most dreadful,' said Mr. Crawford.

'One thing to be said in Dhung's favour,' said Major Minnies, 'he *was* a fool. It's worse when they're not. Like our Friend. When they are so well endowed by nature with looks, brains, personality, everything: and *then* to see them go to pot … What is it, dear lady? You're leaving us?'

1 **sort**: type of person 6 **hullaballoo**: big excitement 7 **hotch-potch**: mixture of different things that don't belong together **pepper pot**: Pfefferstreuer 7–8 **Doric column**: altgriechische Säule 8 **HH**: His Highness 11 **have the heck of a time** (infml): es verdammt schwer haben 15 **inaugurate sth.**: etwas einweihen
16 **pour your tale**: tell sth. important **woe** (old-fashioned): worries, distress
17 **fuddy-duddy** (infml, derog): person with old-fashioned ideas 27 **be endowed with sth.**: have sth. (e.g. a particular feature or quality) 28 **go to pot** (infml): become ruined or decadent

'To your brandy and cigars.'

The three men were on their feet, watching her walk across the moonlit lawn. She went into the house but not into the drawing-room where the servants were bringing her coffee. She went up on the terrace and leaned thoughtfully on the parapet. She could see the three men still at table down below. Probably now that she had gone they were talking more freely – about the Nawab and his mysterious misdeeds. She felt strange, strange. She looked beyond the little tableau in her garden of three Englishmen in dinner jackets blowing smoke from their cigars while the servants hovered around them with decanters: she had a moonlight view of the Saunders' house, then the spire of the little church and the graves in the cemetery, and beyond that the flat landscape she knew so well, those miles of dun earth that led to Khatm.

* * * *

12 June. I keep getting letters from Chid. I was surprised on receiving the first one as I did not think he was the type to look back and remember people. The letter started off not with a personal salutation but in black letters: *Jai Shiva Shankar! Hari Om!* He wrote: 'It is the light around our body that controlls our mind. A pure true un-harmfull mind is a place of perfect HAPPINESS. So it is the perfect PURE TRUE and UN-harmfull mind – that is Heaven.' It went on like that for most of the letter except that somewhere in the middle he wrote 'We are here in Y Dharmsala. A Pure place except the priest who tries to cheat and rob us.' And at the end there was another line: 'I forgott my drinking mug send care Y Sri Krishna Maharaj Temple Dharmsala by *registered* post express.'

His subsequent letters conformed to the same pattern: a lot of philosophy with somewhere in the middle a couple of factual lines (usually to do with being 'cheated and robbed') and at the end a request. They

5 **parapet**: low wall 10 **hover around sb.**: um jdn. herumschwirren **decanter**: special bottle to pour alcohol 11 **spire**: Turmspitze 13 **dun**: of greyish, brownish colour 17 **Hari Om**: Praise to the Lord (form of Indian greeting) 22 **Dharmsala**: mountain town in north India, famous place for pilgrimages 26 **subsequent**: later, following

are interesting documents and I am keeping them, with Olivia's letters, on my little desk. They make strange company together. Olivia's handwriting is clear and graceful, even though she seems to have written very fast just as the thoughts and feelings came to her. Her letters are all addressed to Marcia, but really they sound as if she is communing with herself, they are so intensely personal. Chid's letters are absolutely impersonal. And he always writes on those impersonal post office forms which seem to constitute, along with stained and illegible postcards, the bulk of the mail that crosses from one end of India to the other. They always look as if they have been travelling great distances and passed through many hands, absorbing many stains and smells along the way. Olivia's letters – more than fifty years old – look as if they had been written yesterday. It is true, the ink is faint but this may have been the quality she used to blend with the delicate lilac colour and scent of her stationery. The scent still seems to linger. Chid's crumpled letters, on the other hand, appear soaked in all the characteristic odours of India, in spices, urine, and betel.

Inder Lal is always eager to hear Chid's letters. He comes up to my room in the evenings so that I can read them out to him. He likes all that philosophy. He tells me that Chid's is a very old soul which has passed through many incarnations. Most of them have been in India and that is why Chid has come back in this birth. But what Inder Lal doesn't understand is why *I* have come. He doesn't think I was Indian in any previous birth, so why should I come in this one?

I try to find an explanation for him. I tell him that many of us are tired of the materialism of the West, and even if we have no particular attraction towards the spiritual message of the East, we come here in the hope of finding a simpler and more natural way of life. This explanation hurts him. He feels it to be a mockery. He says why should people who have everything – motor cars, refrigerators – come here to such a place where there is nothing? He says he often feels ashamed before me

5 **commune with sb.** (fml): share your emotions and feelings with sb.
8 **constitute sth.**: make up sth. **stained** (adj) fleckig 8–9 **the bulk of sth.**: the main part of sth. 14 **blend sth.**: mix sth. 15 **linger**: stay on **crumple sth.**: etwas verknittern 16 **odour** (fml): smell 21 **incarnation**: Wiedergeburt
22 **birth**: (here) life 29 **mockery**: Spott

because of the way he is living. When I try to protest, he works himself up more. He says he is perfectly well aware that, by Western standards, his house as well as his food and his way of eating it would be considered primitive, inadequate – indeed, he himself would be considered so because of his unscientific mind and ignorance of the modern world. Yes he knows very well that he is lagging far behind in all these respects and on that account I am well entitled to laugh at him. Why shouldn't I laugh! he cries, not giving me a chance to say anything – he himself often feels like laughing when he looks around him and sees the conditions in which people are living and the superstitions in their minds. Who would not laugh, he says, pointing out of the window where one of the town's beggars happens to be passing, a teenage boy who cannot stand upright but drags the crippled underpart of his body behind him in the dust – who would not laugh, asks Inder Lal, to see a sight like that?

At such times I remember Karim and Kitty. I had gone to see them in London just before coming out to India. Karim is the Nawab's nephew and heir, and Kitty, his wife, is also of some Indian royal (or rather, ex-royal) house. When I phoned Karim and told him I was going to India to do some research into the history of Khatm, he asked me round to their flat in Knightsbridge. He himself opened the door: 'Hi there,' he said. He was an extremely handsome young man, dressed in the height of London boutique fashion. I kept wondering whether he resembled the Nawab at all. Probably not, as Karim is very slender, almost slight, with delicate features and long curly hair; whereas the Nawab in his prime is said to have been a well set-up man with a strong, rather hawk-like face.

Karim ushered me into a room full of people. At first I thought it was a party but afterwards realised that they had just dropped in. They were Karim and Kitty's set. Most of them were sitting on the floor which was

1–2 **work yourself up**: get angry or excited 7 **on that account**: because of that **be entitled to**: have the right 10 **superstition**: Aberglaube 21 **Knightsbridge**: wealthy area in west London 23 **resemble sb./sth.**: look like sb./sth. 24 **slender**: gracefully thin **slight**: small and thin, not strong 25–26 **in his prime**: in der Blüte seiner Jahre 26 **hawk**: Falke 28 **usher sb.**: take or show sb. where to go 30 **set** (n): group of friends or people who spend a lot of time together

strewn with cushions, bolsters, and rugs. Everything was Indian, including most of the people there. They had a tape playing of sarod music – no one was listening but it made a good background to their talk which was carried on in high-pitched, rather bird-like voices. Kitty was curled up on a red and gold sofa which had once been a swing and was fixed to the ceiling by long golden chains. She too was dressed in smart London casual clothes – pants and a silk shirt – and wore them as gracefully as a sari: this may have been the effect of her very slender limbs, waist, and neck, combined with hips of a surprising voluptuousness. She too said 'Hi there,' and then she waved her hand vaguely around the room, murmuring 'Take a pew.'

I never did make out who they all were and whether they were all living in London or were just visiting. I had an impression that they commuted rather freely and sometimes I didn't know whether they were talking about something that had happened in Bombay or in London They seemed to be engaged in a lot of selling and spoke knowingly about which family treasures could be safely carried out of India in one's hand baggage and which had to be got over by other means.

The only English people there besides myself were a couple called Keith and Doreen. They looked larger, stronger, coarser than the other people in the room and were listening eagerly – even, it seemed to me, greedily – to the conversation about family treasures. They told me that they were designers and were about to go into the manufacture of boutique clothes made exclusively of Indian materials. They were starting a partnership with Kitty and Karim: Karim would be helping them with their contacts and Kitty was to come in on the creative side. She was, they said, very creative.

Karim had curled up on a cushion at my feet. He looked up at me with his beautiful eyes and said 'You must tell us about your research.' When I said that I was especially interested in his uncle, the previous Nawab, he said 'Wasn't he a naughty boy?' Everyone laughed; they said that there had been a lot of naughty boys in those days. They began to

1 **be strewn with sth.**: be covered with sth. **bolster**: thick pillow shaped like a long tube 2 **sarod**: Indian string instrument, smaller than the sitar 5 **swing**: Schaukel 8 **limb**: arm or leg 9 **voluptuousness**: state of having a full and round figure 11 **pew**: (here) seat 20 **coarse**: grob 22 **greedy**: gierig

tell stories. They all seemed to have relatives who had been involved in scandals in London hotels, had been deposed for some frightful misdemeanour, had squandered away family fortunes, had died of drink, drugs, or poison administered by illegitimate brothers. They spoke of these matters with nostalgia: 'Say what you like,' concluded one of them, 'those days had their own charm.'

From there they passed on to a discussion of present days which had no charm at all. India was of course home but was becoming so impossible to live in that they had to stay mostly abroad. Yet all of them were eager to serve India and would have done so if it had not been for the intransigent attitude of the present government. They had many bad experiences to relate on this score. One girl told how her family had tried to turn their palace into a hotel. It was in a beautiful picturesque area with many items of tourist interest all around, and some foreign investors had been very interested in the venture. But the Government of India wanted licences for everything and then refused to issue the licences. For instance, the palace was old, it had been built in the nineteenth century and, naturally, to make it convenient for modern tourists all sorts of modern sanitary fittings would have had to be imported. You could hardly, she said, expect a modern tourist to sit on a thunderbox! But try and explain that simple point to a Secretary of the Government of India who knows only one word which is no. In the end the foreign investors had got discouraged and had gone elsewhere. Now the palace was just lying there deserted with the roof caving in, so that the family had had no alternative but to get all their stuff out for auction abroad. There had been some priceless things – including a golden chariot in which the Lord Krishna was taken out in procession once a year – and they *had* fetched a good price: but of course, as everyone knew, there were so many middlemen to be paid off – the dealers and

2–3 **misdemeanour** [ˌmɪsdɪˈmiːnə] (fml): minor wrongdoing 3 **squander away sth.**: waste sth. carelessly 4 **administer sth. to sb.** (fml): give sth. (e.g. medicine, drugs) to sb. 11 **intransigent**: unnachgiebig 12 **on this score**: about this, related to this 15 **venture**: Unternehmen, Wagnis 16 **issue sth.**: give sth. (e.g. an official document) 21 **thunderbox**: Donnerbalken, Plumpsklo **Secretary**: Minister 23 **get discouraged**: lose confidence or interest 24 **cave in**: collapse 27 **chariot**: Streitwagen **Krishna**: one of the incarnations of the God Vishnu

the auctioneers and the people who arranged for the things to go out of India.

Karim told me that he had also had to get rid of most of the treasures in the palace at Khatm. If they had been left there, they would have been ruined by white ants and fungus. There had been a large collection of miniature paintings, but no one had cared about it; it had never been catalogued and was kept wrapped in sheets in underground chambers. Now fortunately most of it had been sold to foreign buyers, though Karim had kept some pictures – not so much for their value as for family associations.

'Come, I will show you.' He jumped up, gracefully unwinding his long legs, and led me into another room. This one seemed like a charming, rather exotic sitting room, full of rugs and painted furniture, but Karim said it was just the filthy little old den where he and Kitty liked to come and relax. It was here – framed in gold on the red wallpaper of Kitty and Karim's den – that I had my first sight of the palace at Khatm. It looked different from the way it does now, but this may have been due to the stylisation of the artist. Everything was jewelled: the flowers in the garden, the drops of water in the fountain.

The pictures showed princes and princesses engaged in various pleasurable pursuits. The princes looked like Karim, the princesses like Kitty. They all wore a great deal of jewellery. Karim told me that most of the family jewellery had disappeared long ago – as a matter of fact, he said, smiling, it was the Nawab I was interested in who had been largely responsible for its disappearance. He had always needed money and hadn't cared how he laid his hands on it. He had led rather a riotous life – there had been all sorts of scandals – even (perhaps I had heard?) with an Englishwoman in India, the wife of an I.C.S. officer.

'Yes,' I said and passed on to the next picture. This, Karim explained, was the founder of their line, Amanullah Khan (he who had taken refuge

5 **fungus**: (Schimmel)pilz 7 **catalogue sth.**: list sth. in a catalogue giving details about it **wrap sth.**: etwas einwickeln 9–10 **for family associations**: wegen der Verbindung mit der Familie 11 **unwind sth.** [ˌʌnwaɪnd]: etwas entfalten 16 **den**: Versteck 21 **pursuit**: leisure activity 26 **riotous**: exciting and enjoyable in an uncontrolled way 28 **ICS = Imperial Civil Service**: the British administration in India

with Baba Firdaus). He looked respectable enough in the picture – in a flowered gown, a pink turban, a long moustache, and smoking a hookah: but, Karim said, it showed him at the end of his life when he had been confirmed in his conquests by treaty with the East India Company. Before that he had lived mostly in the saddle, with few possessions beyond his sword and a band of followers as rough as himself.

'Oh he was a character!' said Karim, speaking of Amanullah Khan with the same admiration as the Nawab had always done. 'He was very short and squat and had bandy legs from always sitting on a horse. Everyone was terrified of him on account of his frightful temper. He got very quarrelsome while drinking and once, when one of his drinking companions contradicted something he'd said, he got so angry he took his sword and cut off the poor guy's arm. Just like that, with one stroke. *Wow*. There are lots of stories about him and people still sing songs about him – folk songs and such. The family's been there since 1817 which is when we became the Nawabs, and if I ever care to stand for Parliament, they'd return me like a shot. Sometimes I think I would like to – after all, one is Indian and wants to serve the country and all that – but you know, whenever we go to Khatm, Kitty gets a stomach upset due to the water. And of course there is no proper doctor there so what are we to do, we have to get back to the hotel in Bombay as quickly as possible. But now we're thinking of buying an apartment in Bombay because of this business we are starting with Keith and Doreen. Kitty has done a lot of research on ancient Indian paintings from Ajanta and such places which are fabulous and her designs will be based on these so, you see, we will be serving our country, won't we, through the export-import business?'

He looked at me with eyes which were deep and yearning (rather like Inder Lal's, I was to discover later). I didn't meet him again after that one visit, and though I sometimes think of him here, it is difficult to fit him and Kitty in either at Khatm or at Satipur; or even what I saw of Bombay.

2 **gown**: garment worn over other clothes **hookah**: Wasserpfeife 4 **confirm sb. in sth.**: jdm. etwas bestätigen 9 **squat**: short and thick **bandy**: (of legs) curving outwards so that the knees are wide apart 11 **quarrelsome**: fond of starting angry arguments 17 **like a shot**: very quickly 28 **yearning** (adj): sehnsüchtig

1923

It was now no longer Harry who came to fetch Olivia but just the car and chauffeur. Harry was not keeping good health. He said he could not stand the heat nor the food from the Nawab's kitchen. He always had some stomach complaint, even though the Nawab had undertaken the ordering of his meals himself and only the European-trained chef was allowed to prepare them. But none of it seemed to agree with Harry.

He stayed mostly in his own suite of rooms, and Olivia visited him there. But he was not in a good mood with her. Once he even said to her, quite abruptly, 'Douglas doesn't know you come to Khatm, does he?' and before she could recover herself, he said further 'You shouldn't keep coming. You shouldn't be here.'

'That's what Douglas says about you,' she replied. 'But it seems to me you're not so badly off here really.'

She cast a glance at his surroundings to show what she meant. The Nawab had given his best guest suite to Harry. It was a suite of marble rooms with latticed windows looking out over the fountains and rose gardens. It had been charmingly furnished for Harry with some very fine pieces of European furniture. Only the pictures on the walls were Indian. They came from the Nawab's family collection of miniatures and were mostly of an erotic nature – princes sporting in bowers, princesses being prepared for nuptial delights.

Harry said 'Have you noticed something? That you're never taken to meet the Begum and her ladies?'

'I *have* met them, thank you.' She gave a forced laugh: 'It was hard going.'

'Nevertheless,' said Harry, 'it's a discourtesy.'

'To whom?'

'To you, to you.'

They were both silent, then he said: 'I've had a quarrel with him about it ... about you. I asked him straight out –'

5 **stomach complaint**: Magenbeschwerden 7 **agree with sb.**: jdm. gut bekommen 14 **be not badly off**: be not in a really bad situation 15 **cast a glance at sb./sth.**: take a quick look at sb./sth. 21 **sport** (v): play in a happy and lively way **bower**: Laube 22 **nuptial**: ehelich 27 **discourtesy**: behaviour that is not polite

'What?'

'"Why aren't you taking Olivia – Mrs. Rivers – to meet the Begum?" He –'

'What?' she asked again.

'Oh,' said Harry, 'you know how he can be when he doesn't want to answer something. He laughs, and if you keep on he makes you feel a fool and prim and stupid for asking such questions. He's very good at that.'

'I don't *want* to meet the Begum,' she said, playing with her bracelet. She continued: 'I come here to be with you – and him of course – I mean, as your friend. Both of you. I can't be friends with them, can I. Not with someone who doesn't speak the same language ... I enjoy being here. I enjoy your company. We have a good time. Don't look like that, Harry. You're being like everyone else now: making me feel I don't *understand*. That I don't know India. It's true I don't, but what's that got to do with it? People can still be friends, can't they, even if it is India.' She said all this in a rush; she didn't want to be answered, she was stating her position which she felt to be right. Next she asked: 'What is all this about dacoits, Harry? ... Tell me,' she said when he didn't.

He sighed, and after a while he said 'Honestly I don't know, Olivia. A lot of things go on and I'd just as soon not know about them. Gosh but I feel ill. Awful.'

'Is it your stomach?'

'That too. And this dashed, dashed heat.'

'It's *cool* in here. It's lovely.'

'But outside, outside!' He shut his eyes.

She went to the window. The sun was beating down of course – the gold dome of the Nawab's mosque gave out blinding beams – but the lawns were sparkling green and the fountains, refracting the sun's rays, dazzled with light and water. In the distance, beyond the pearl-grey Palace walls, lay the town in a miserable stretch of broken roofs, and beyond that the barren land: but why look that far?

7 **prim**: prüde 21 **gosh** (infml): expression of annoyance or surprise 24 **dashed** (old-fashioned infml): verflixt 29 **refract sth.**: make sth. (esp. light) change direction when it goes through an angle 30 **dazzle**: blenden

The Nawab came in – on tiptoe: 'I'm not disturbing? Please say if I am and I shall run away at once.' He looked with searching concern at Harry, then, turned to Olivia: 'How do you find him? What do you think? I have called in doctors but he does not like our Indian doctors. He thinks they are – what do you think, Harry?'

'Quacks.'

'Ridiculous,' smiled the Nawab. 'Dr. Puri from Chhatra Bazaar has a degree from Ludhiana College – he is a very highly qualified person –'

'He's a witch doctor,' Harry said.

'Ridiculous,' smiled the Nawab again. He sat on the edge of the sofa on which Harry was resting. 'We want you to get well again quickly, quickly. We miss you. It is very dull without you – isn't it, Olivia?' And he turned right round now to look at her, as if to gather her up too within the shelter of his fondness and care.

'She's been asking about the dacoits,' Harry said.

As the Nawab's eyes were at that moment so fully looking into hers, she saw an expression in them which he might normally have taken care to hide. And for a few seconds longer he searched her face. Then he turned away.

He said in a mild voice: 'I hope, Olivia, whenever you wish to know something – if something is strange to you – that at such times you will ask not Harry, nor some other person, but myself only.' He leaned forward: 'Who has spoken to you? What have they said? No you must tell me. If you don't tell me, how can I defend myself against the slanders people may bring against me. You must give me this chance.'

Harry said 'What are you asking her to do – bring you reports from the Civil Lines at Satipur? Be your spy?'

The Nawab leaned back again. He lowered his eyes as if in shame. He said in a humble voice 'I hope you don't believe this of me, Olivia.'

She cried out at once 'Of course not! How could you think it!' and looked reproachfully at Harry.

6 **quack** (infml): Quacksalber 8 **degree**: academic qualification 24 **slander**: false statement to damage sb.'s reputation 29 **humble** (adj): not proud 31 **reproachful**: vorwurfsvoll

On Sunday evenings Douglas and Olivia usually took a stroll through the graveyard. They wandered arm in arm along the paths between the graves, stopping to read the inscriptions so that the names of the dead became familiar to them. Olivia called these Sunday excursions their visiting rounds, but Douglas was apologetic about them. He said it was a shame that all the entertainment he could offer her was a walk around a graveyard. 'Think of Marcia,' he said ruefully, 'in gay Paree.'

'Silly.' She pressed his arm. 'Where do you think I'd rather be.'

They were standing by the grave of a young lieutenant – E.A. Edwards of the 54th who had fallen with five of his brother officers at the head of his regiment on 11 May 1857. Aged 29 years. He had become a particular friend because Olivia liked the inscription: *As a soldier ever ready where Duty called him, a dutiful son, a kind and indulgent Father but most conspicuous in the endearing character of Husband . . .*

'Just like you, darling,' she told Douglas, pressing his arm again. After a while she added 'Except you're not a kind and indulgent father yet.'

'But I will be,' he promised.

'Of course you will.'

The fact was, however, that she was not getting pregnant. She was beginning to be worried: was something wrong? She could not believe it; she was sure that a couple like herself and Douglas were meant to have children, to be the founders of a beautiful line. He too was sure of it. Sometimes she thought it might be due to psychological reasons – because she had been so frightened by all the little babies in the graveyard, dead of smallpox, dead of cholera, dead of enteric fever.

She had brought a few flowers for the Saunders' baby. She knelt to place them at the feet of the Italian angel. When she got up, her face was radiant; she took Douglas' arm and whispered into his ear 'I made a wish ... You know, the way they do at Baba Firdaus' shrine on the Husband's Wedding Day.' They both smiled, but then she became serious and asked 'Douglas, what *is* this thing about dacoits?'

1 **stroll** (n): slow casual walk 7 **rueful**: reuevoll **Paree**: (imitation of French pronunciation) Paris 13 **indulgent**: nachsichtig 14 **conspicuous**: remarkable 25 **smallpox**: Pocken **enteric fever**: Typhus 28 **radiant** ['reɪdiənt]: shining and glowing

'There is a gang operating around Khatm. They've been terrorising the outlying villages – making raids and looting and some killings too.'

'How dreadful.' She added 'But what's *he* got to do with it?'

'Our Friend? That's the point. He's generally thought to be in cahoots with them, getting a rake-off in return for his protection.'

'It couldn't be,' said Olivia.

Douglas laughed at her innocence. They walked on. He pointed out a few more Mutiny graves, but she was no longer interested.

She said 'But he's a *ruler*. He wouldn't get himself mixed up with a robber gang like that. After all he *is* a prince.' When Douglas burst out laughing, she said in a rather offended voice 'He even has some sort of English title.'

'Oh yes he's got all sorts of things … Look, here's another one killed on 11 May '57: *Lt. Peter John Lisle of Clifton, Bristol*. He must have fallen in the same action as Lt. Edwards. There was an uprising in Satipur inspired by the then Raja of Satipur who had joined the mutineers: for which he paid very dearly afterwards. Unlike his neighbour at Khatm, our Friend's great-grandfather, who remained 'loyal': *after* making sure which was the best side to remain loyal to. That's how he got his English title and all his other perks. Clever chap.' He carefully picked a few weeds out of Lt. Lisle's grave. There were not many – the graves were extremely well kept. A permanent watchman had been hired, and Mr. Crawford himself came regularly for inspection to make sure the English dead were paid the respect due to them.

'Quite apart from anything else,' Olivia said, watching Douglas pick weeds, 'he wouldn't *need* to, would he, join a gang of robbers. It's ridiculous. I mean, after all, he must be a rich man … Do stop that.'

'But they're weeds.'

'Oh goodness, let's go. This place is getting me down.'

Douglas got up and dusted the knees of his trousers. Now he looked rather offended; he said 'I thought you said you liked it here.'

2 **raid**: Überfall **looting** (n): Plünderung 4–5 **be in cahoots with sb.** (infml): be doing sth. illegal together with sb. 5 **rake-off** (infml): a share of profits from illegal activity 15 **uprising** (n): rebellion 16 **mutineer**: Meuterer 20 **perk**: an advantage or benefit received (from your employer) 21 **weed**: Unkraut

'I like the trees.'

She turned and walked away from him down a path. She didn't want him to see how irritated she was both with him and the dead heroes. But she had more to ask him, so she stopped still and waited for him to catch up. 'What sort of dacoits?' she asked.

'I don't want to talk about it.' Douglas wore his stuffy look. He stared in front of him like a soldier on parade. He was making straight for the exit.

Now it was Olivia who lingered behind. She stopped again by the Saunders' grave and knelt to rearrange her flowers. She remained there. It was getting darker, the shadows were gathering. Sadness filled her heart. She didn't know why: perhaps because she wasn't having a baby? She thought if she had a baby – a strapping blond blue-eyed boy – everything would be all right. She would be at peace and also at one with Douglas and think about everything the same way he did.

'Come along now,' Douglas called back to her in a testy voice. 'It's getting dark.'

She got up obediently but next moment – she didn't know how this happened to her – she sank to her knees again and covered her face with her hands. The angel glimmered white above her. The last birds stirred in the tree before falling asleep; otherwise there was no sound. Olivia wept silently. Then she heard Douglas' footsteps crunching along the path as he made his way back to her. But he too was silent as he stood above her, waiting.

'Sorry,' she said after a while. She blew her nose into her handkerchief and wiped her eyes. She got up, but he didn't help her. She looked into his face – she could just make it out in the gathering darkness, glimmering above her like the angel. He stood there stiff and straight; he said 'You should have gone to Simla. The heat's getting you down.'

'Is that what it is,' she said, glad of the excuse.

* * * *

6 **wear sth.**: have sth. (esp. a particular expression or look) on your face **stuffy**: formal and boring 13 **strapping** (adj): big, tall, strong 16 **testy**: bad tempered 20 **glimmer**: schimmern 22 **crunch**: knirschen

15 June. One of the town's beggars is a very old woman: at least she looks very old, but this may be due to her life of deprivation. She doesn't ask for alms, but when she is hungry she stands there with her hand stretched out. I never see her talk to anyone. Although she stays in the town, she does not seem to have a permanent pitch anywhere. Sometimes I see her in the Civil Lines area, sometimes by the royal tombs, sometimes in the bazaar or the alleys around it. She shuffles about in her rags, and when she is tired she squats or lies wherever she happens to be and people passing have to walk around her.

For the past few days, however, I have been seeing her in the same place. There is an alley behind our house where our washerman lives (the same alley where I saw the eunuchs dance). A few days ago I took some clothes to him, and I can't be sure of this but I think she may have been lying there at the time. The trouble is, one is so used to her that one tends not to see her. But I definitely noticed her when I went back to fetch the clothes. There was something about the way she was lying there that drew my attention. The lane ends in a piece of land where a man lives in a shed with two buffaloes. Just outside his shed the municipality have put up a concrete refuse dump, but most people see no point in throwing their refuse within the concrete enclosure so that it lies littered around it, forming a little mound. The reason why I noticed the beggar woman was because she was lying on the outskirts of this mound of refuse. I thought at first she was dead but realised this could not be since no one else in the lane seemed concerned. The animals snuffling around in the refuse also paid no attention to her. Only the flies hovered above her in a cone.

The washerman was not at home and his wife was very busy with her household chores as well as pushing a long wooden pole into the clothes that had been put to boil. When I mentioned the presence of the beggar

2 **deprivation**: Entbehrung 3 **alms** (pl): Almosen 5 **pitch**: (here) place where a person can often be found 7 **shuffle**: walk without lifting your feet completely off the ground 8 **squat**: hocken 18 **shed**: Schuppen, Stall 18–19 **municipality**: local government 19 **refuse dump**: Müllhalde 20 **enclosure**: piece of land surrounded by a wall 21 **littered**: (of rubbish) left around a place so that it is untidy **mound**: small hill 22 **outskirts** (pl): an area away from the centre of sth. 25 **snuffle**: schnüffeln 26 **cone**: Kegel 28 **pole**: Stange, Stab

woman, she had no time to listen to me. Neither had the coalman who lives in an opening in the adjoining wall, nor the man with the buffaloes. They murmured vaguely when I asked how long she had been there. It struck me that perhaps she *was* dead and it was no one's business to take her away. Not mine either, and I went home carrying my laundry.

Later I wondered what had happened to me – that I had not even bothered to go close to see whether she was alive or dead. I told Inder Lal about her, but he was busy getting ready to leave for his office. I wanted him to come with me to see her so I followed him when he started off. He was wheeling his cycle with his tiffin carrier tied to the handlebar. Although he was very reluctant, I persuaded him to enter the alley with me. I saw at once that she was still there. We stopped to look at her from a distance. 'Is she alive?' I asked him. He didn't know and was not inclined to investigate; anyway, it was time for him to go, he could not be late to the office. I decided I had to see. I stepped closer – Inder Lal cried 'No don't!' and even rang the bell of his cycle as a warning. I went up to the refuse dump, I stood over the beggar woman: her eyes were open, she was groaning, she was alive. There was a terrible smell and a cluster of flies. I looked down and saw a thin stream of excrement trickling out of her. My first thought was for Inder Lal: I made gestures to him to go away, go to his office. I was glad he had remained at a distance. I gestured more wildly and was relieved when he turned away – clean in his much washed clothes and with his freshly cooked food in his tiffin carrier. I walked away, and when I passed the coal merchant, I said 'She is ill.' He assented vaguely. The washerman could be seen through the arched doorway eating his food in his courtyard. I could not disturb him. In fact, I felt I could not disturb or go near anyone. For the first time I understood – I *felt* – the Hindu fear of pollution. I went home and bathed rigorously, rinsing myself over and over again. I was

3 **murmur**: say sth. in a low voice 10 **wheel sth.**: push sth. (that has wheels) **tiffin carrier** (IndE): lunch box 11 **handlebar**: Lenkstange **reluctant**: unwilling, hesitating 14 **inclined** (adj): geneigt 18 **groan**: make a deep sad sound when in pain 19 **excrement**: Kot 20 **trickle**: flow in a thin stream 25 **assent**: express agreement 28 **pollution**: Verschmutzung, Verunreinigung 29 **rigorous**: harsh **rinse sth.**: wash sth. with clean water

afraid. Pollution – infection – seemed everywhere; those flies could easily have carried it from her to me.

Later I went to the local hospital situated at the Civil Lines end of town. It is an old, grim stone building – the same one Dr. Saunders was in charge of – and it is too small for the town's needs. In-patients and out-patients overflowed on to the verandahs and corridors and the patch of grass outside. I went straight into the Medical Superintendent's room which was large, airy, and tidy. The Medical Superintendent, Dr. Gopal, was also tidy – a goodlooking man in a white coat and an oiled moustache. He was very polite, even gallant, and got up from behind his desk to greet me and seat me in the chair facing him. The desk and chairs were solid old pieces of English furniture, probably dating from the time of Dr. Saunders. Dr. Gopal was very sympathetic to my story and said, if I would bring her in, they would see what could be done. When I asked whether it would be possible to have her brought in an ambulance, he said that unfortunately the ambulance was under repair and in any case it was only meant for cases of emergency.

'But she *is* an emergency.'

The doctor smiled sadly and stroked his moustache. He asked me the standard question: 'Which country you are from?' Although no doubt a very busy man, he seemed prepared to talk to me longer. I had the impression that he wanted to, perhaps in order to practise his English.

Two out-patients came in, bearing slips of paper. They were villagers with simple faces under big turbans; they stretched out the slips of paper to Dr. Gopal. Under his brusque questioning, it soon transpired that the two prescriptions had got mixed up, and that Meher Chand who was suffering from piles was taking the medicine meant for Bacchu Ram who had gallstones. Dr. Gopal quickly rectified this mistake and dismissed the patients who left looking satisfied.

4 **grim**: depressing, unattractive 5 **in-patient**: stationäre/r Patient/in 6 **out-patient**: ambulante/r Patient/in 7 **superintendent**: person who manages, controls and supervises a place, etc. 19 **stroke sth.**: etwas streicheln 26 **brusque**: using a few words in an abrupt way **transpire**: become known 27 **prescription**: Rezept 28 **piles**: Hämorrhoiden 29 **gallstone**: Gallenstein **rectify sth.**: correct sth., put sth. right

I asked 'Does it happen very often?'

'Of course. These people can't read and the orderlies are not very careful. You see our problem. If she is dying,' he said, 'then don't bring her, there is not much we can do.'

'But then where should she die?'

'You see our problem,' he said again. 'There has been no addition to the hospital for over twenty years. We don't have beds, we don't have staff or equipment.' He went on. It was a long list of difficulties. Again I saw that he liked talking to me – partly to practise his English, that motive may have been there, but also to have someone to whom he could in this way unburden himself. 'You saw the type of patients we have, and then also we make mistakes on our side, how is it to be avoided? I would like to have more staff, I make applications in triplicate, I go to see the Minister: at last when I get the staff, they are often useless people.' His English was fluent and he expressed himself well. He had a lot to express – his feelings were deep and his life difficult. He looked at me across the desk with the same eyes as Inder Lal's, craving understanding.

What I understood best was that the problem of the beggar woman, if I wished to undertake it, was now mine. Everyone else had too many problems of their own. I thought what to do. Perhaps she could still be treated and, on that chance, I had to get her to the hospital. I could hire a cycle rickshaw or a horse carriage to take her there. Then I thought how to get her into a vehicle. I would have to lift her by myself, for I could not expect anyone else to take the risk of touching her; also, I was not at all sure whether I could persuade any carriage owner to take her.

I made my way from Dr. Gopal's office through the crowded hospital corridors. I kept having to step over patients lying on the floor. 'Then where should she die?' I had asked Dr. Gopal. It had seemed a forceful question to me at the time, but now it no longer was so. Now a new thought – a new word – presented itself to me, and it was this: that the old woman was *dispensable*. I was surprised at myself. I realised I was

2 **orderly**: Pfleger(in) 6 **addition**: Erweiterung 11 **unburden oneself**: sich etwas von der Seele reden 13 **triplicate**: consisting of three copies 17 **crave sth.**: have a strong desire for sth. 32 **dispensable**: entbehrlich

changing, becoming more like everyone else. But also I thought that, if one lives here, it is best to be like everyone else. Perhaps there is even no choice: everything around me – the people and the landscape, life animate and inanimate – seemed to compel me into this attitude.

Walking back from the hospital, I passed Maji's hut near the royal tombs. She was sitting outside and beckoned to me. She looked into my face and asked me what was the matter. I told her; by this time I spoke of it with the same indifference as everyone else. But I was startled by Maji's reaction which was not at all like everyone else's. 'What?' she cried. 'Leelavati? Her time has come?' Leelavati! The beggar woman had a name! Suddenly the whole thing became urgent again. Maji scrambled up and dashed off in the direction of the bazaar with amazing speed for one so stout and elderly. I hurried behind her, to lead her to the garbage dump. But when we got there, the beggar woman had gone. We asked the washerman, the coal merchant, the buffalo owner: all shrugged as before and said she had gone somewhere else. They thought she must have got hungry and dragged herself off to beg for food. I felt foolish, having made so much fuss.

But Maji said 'I know where she may be.' Again she set off at the same trot, sticking out her elbows to steer herself more quickly. We hurried back to the bazaar, then through the gate leading out of town till we came to the reservoir with the suttee stones on its bank. 'Ah!' cried Maji. She had seen her before I did. She was lying under a tree in the same way she had been lying by the garbage dump. The stream of excrement was still flowing out of her but only in the thinnest trickle now. Maji went up to her and said 'There you are. I have been looking for you. Why didn't you call me?' The old woman was staring into the sky but it seemed to me her eyes were already sightless. Maji sat down under a tree and took the old woman's head into her lap. She stroked it with her thick peasant hands and looked down into the dying face. Suddenly the old woman smiled, her toothless mouth opened with the

4 **compel sb.**: force sb. 6 **beckon to sb.**: make a gesture to sb. to tell them sth. 11–12 **scramble up**: sich aufrappeln 12 **dash off**: rush, move quickly 13 **stout** [staʊt]: rather fat 15 **shrug**: mit den Schultern zucken 19–20 **at the same trot**: mit denselben schnellen, kleinen Schritten 20 **steer sb./sth.**: move sb./sth in a particular direction 28 **sightless**: unable to see; blind

same bliss of recognition as a baby's. Were her eyes not yet sightless – could she see Maji looking down at her? Or did she only feel her love and tenderness? Whatever it was, that smile seemed like a miracle to me.

I sat with them under the tree. There had been a particularly severe dust storm earlier in the day and, as sometimes happens, it had cleared the air, so that now, for the remaining hour of daylight, everything was luminous. The water in the reservoir was pure as the sky, disturbed only by the reflections of skimming kingfishers or of trees momentarily nodding their leaves into its surface. At the far end some buffaloes were bathing, immersed so deeply that only their heads were visible above the water. There were a lot of skinny, lively monkeys skipping about on the bank, in and out and over the suttee stones.

'You see,' said Maji, 'I knew she would come here.' She continued to stroke the old woman's face, not only with tenderness but with a sort of pride too; yes really as if she were proud of her for having done something special. She began to tell me about the old woman's life: how she had been left a widow and had been driven out of her father-in-law's house. Next her parents and brother had died in a smallpox epidemic, leaving her homeless and destitute. Then what could she do, Maji said: having been literally thrown on to the world to beg a living from it. At that time she had stayed not in one place but had gone all over, mostly from one pilgrim spot to the other because those were the most rewarding for beggars. About ten years ago she had come to the town and fallen sick here. She recovered but was never again strong enough to move on, so she had just stayed.

'But now she is tired,' said Maji. 'Now it is time. Now she has done enough.' And again she stroked her face and again with pride as if the old woman had acquitted herself well.

It was pleasant sitting here – cool by the water – and we were ready to stay many hours. But she did not keep us waiting long. As the glow

1 **bliss**: great happiness, joy 3 **tenderness**: kindness 5 **severe**: intense, strong
8 **luminous**: bright 9 **skim**: über das Wasser gleiten **kingfisher**: Eisvogel
10 **nod**: move up and down in the wind 11 **immerse sth.**: etwas eintauchen
12 **skip**: jump lightly 20 **destitute**: mittellos 29 **acquit yourself well**: do well in a difficult situation

faded and sky and air and water turned pale silver and the birds fell asleep in the dark trees and now only soundless bats flitted black across the silver sky: at that lovely hour she died. I would not have noticed, for she had not moved for a long time. There was no death rattle or convulsion. It was as if everything had already been squeezed out of her and there was nothing left for her to do except pass over. Maji was very pleased: she said Leelavati had done well and had been rewarded with a good, a blessed end.

1923

One day Olivia told Douglas that Harry was lying ill at Khatm and that she wanted to go and visit him. Douglas said 'Oh?' and nothing further. She took this as the permission she wanted: from now on, she decided, Douglas *knew* that she went to Khatm, she had told him, he was apprised of the facts. There would be no need in future to hurry back lest he arrive at home before her. If he did, she could simply and truthfully tell him that she had been to visit sick Harry at Khatm. But he never did arrive before her; somehow he seemed to be kept at the office later and later, and when he came home he was so tired that he went to sleep very soon. Olivia stayed up much later, sitting by the window to catch some cool air. She was usually still asleep when he left in the morning; he always left very early so as to be able to ride out on inspection before the sun got too hot.

However, one morning she was awake. She came and sat with him in their breakfast room (now the post office); this was something she had not done for some time. She watched him eat ham and sausages. It struck her that his face had become heavier, even somewhat puffy, making him look more like other Englishmen in India. She pushed that thought aside: it was unbearable.

'Douglas,' she said, 'Harry doesn't seem to be getting any better.'

2 **flit**: flattern, huschen 5 **convulsion**: Muskelkrampf **squeeze sth. out of sb.**: etwas aus jdm. herausquetschen 13–14 **apprise sb. of sth.** (fml): inform sb. of sth. 14 **lest** (fml): aus Furcht, dass 26 **puffy**: geschwollen

'Oh?' He had cut up his food into small pieces and was chewing it slowly, stolidly.

'I was wondering whether we shouldn't ask Dr. Saunders to have a look at him.'

'Dr. Saunders doesn't take private patients.'

'But he's the only English doctor around here.' When Douglas did not react, she added 'And Harry *is* English.'

Douglas had finished his breakfast and now lit his morning pipe (he smoked a pipe almost constantly now). He puffed at it as slowly and stolidly as he had eaten. She had always loved him for these qualities – for his imperturbability, his English solidness and strength; his manliness. But now suddenly she thought: what manliness? He can't even get me pregnant.

She cried 'Must you smoke that dashed *pipe*? In this *heat*?'

He stayed calm, knocking ash into an ashtray – carefully, so as not to spill any on the tablecloth. At last he said 'You should have gone to Simla.'

'And do what? Take walks with Mrs. Crawford? Go to the same old boring old dinner parties – oh oh,' she said, burying her face in despair, 'one more of those and I'll lie down and die.'

Douglas failed to respond to this outburst. He went on smoking. It was very quiet in the room. The servants, clearing the breakfast dishes, were also as quiet as could be so as not to disturb the Sahib and Memsahib having a quarrel in English.

After a while Olivia said in a contrite voice 'I don't know what's wrong with me.'

'I told you: it's the heat. No Englishwoman is meant to stand it.'

'You're probably right.' She murmured: 'As a matter of fact, darling, I'd like to consult Dr. Saunders myself.'

He looked at her. His face may have changed, but his eyes had remained as clean and clear as ever.

'Because I'm not –' she looked down shyly, then back into his eyes, 'getting pregnant.'

10 **stolid**: without emotion or interest 11 **imperturbability**: Unerschütterlichkeit **solidness**: state of being strong and reliable 25 **contrite**: reuevoll, zerknirscht

He left his pipe in the ashtray (a servant solicitously knocked it out), then got up and went into their bedroom. She followed him. They clung to each other; she whispered 'I don't want anything to change … I don't want *you* to change.'

'I'm not,' he said.

'No you're not.' But she clung to him tighter. She longed to be pregnant; everything would be all right then – he would not change, she would not change, they would be as planned.

'Wait a while,' he said. 'It'll be all right.'

'You think?'

'I'm sure.'

She leaned on his strong arm and went out with him to the front of the house. Although it was still so early in the morning, the air was stale.

'I wish you'd gone to Simla,' he said.

'Away from you?'

'It's so bad for you here. This awful climate.'

'But I feel fine!' She laughed – because she really did. He pressed her arm in gratitude: 'If I can get away we'll both go.'

'You think you can? … Oh you don't have to for me,' she said. 'I'm quite all right – I don't mind it – really I don't. I'm fine,' she said again.

He exclaimed at her fortitude. He wanted to linger, but his syce stood holding his horse, his peon carried his files, his bearer stood waiting with his solar topee.

'Don't come out,' Douglas said, but she did. She looked up at him as he sat in the saddle and he looked down at her. That morning it was difficult for him to leave.

He said 'I'll have a word with Dr. Saunders about Harry.'

She waved to him for as long as she could still see him. A servant held the door open for her to go back into the house, but she stayed looking out a bit longer. Not in the direction in which Douglas had left,

1 **solicitious** (fml): showing great concern about sb.'s welfare 2–3 **cling to sb./sth.**: hold on tightly to sb./sth. 14 **stale**: not fresh and often badly smelling 19 **gratitude**: desire to express thanks 22 **fortitude**: courage to face difficulties **syce** [saɪs]: Indian servant who looks after horses 23 **peon**: low paid office worker; foot soldier 24 **solar topee**: Tropenhelm

but the other way; towards Khatm, towards the Palace. It did not make any difference as everything was under the same pall of dust. But it was true what she had told Douglas: she felt fine – entirely untroubled by the heat or the murky atmosphere. It was as if there were a little spring welling up inside her that kept her fresh and gay.

Later that morning – she looked at her wrist watch, there was still time before the Nawab's car was to come for her – she walked across to the Saunders' house. But Dr. Saunders had already left for the hospital and there was only Mrs. Saunders. Olivia was surprised to find her out of bed. She was sitting in one of the cavernous rooms staring into an empty fireplace. She told Olivia 'It's not good to let them see you in bed … the servants,' she explained, lowering her voice and with a look towards the door. 'I want to be in bed. It's where I ought to be. But you don't know what goes on in their heads.'

She went on staring into the fireplace (it did not even have a grate) as if she saw haunting visions there. There was something haunted about the room: perhaps this was due to the furnishing which did not belong to the Saunders but had been handed on through several generations of government issue. The prints on the wall had also been there for a long time; they were mostly scenes from the Mutiny, as of Sir Henry Lawrence struck by a bullet in the Lucknow Residency.

'You hear a lot of stories,' Mrs. Saunders said. 'There was one lady in Muzzafarbad or one of those places – she was a lady from Somerset.' She sighed (thinking of the fate of this lady, or of distant Somerset?). 'Her *dhobi*,' Mrs. Saunders whispered, leaning closer to Olivia. 'He was ironing her undies and it must have been too much for him. They're very excitable, it's their constitution. I've heard their spicy food's got something to do with it – I wouldn't know if there's any truth in that but

4 **murky**: dark and unpleasant 6 **wrist watch**: Armbanduhr 10 **cavernous**: large and deep 15 **grate**: Gitter, Feuerrost 16 **haunting**: gespenstisch, quälend **haunted**: believed to be visited by ghosts 19 **government issue**: Zuteilung durch die Regierung 21 **Lucknow Residency**: the seat of the British garrison in Lucknow was under siege for three months; the governor, Sir Henry Lawrence was one of the first casualties 23 **Somerset**: county in England 26 **undies** (pl, infml): underclothes 27 **excitable**: leicht erregbar **constitution**: Konstitution, Verfassung

of this I'm sure, Mrs. Rivers: they've got only one thought in their heads and that's to you-know-what with a white woman.'

Olivia stared back at her. Mrs. Saunders nodded with grim knowledge; she adjusted her dress over her gaunt chest. Olivia found that her hand too had strayed to adjust the rather low neckline of her pale brown silk frock. Ridiculous! She jumped up – it was time to go, the Nawab's car would nearly be there now.

The Nawab laughed at the idea of bringing in Dr. Saunders. He said, if a European doctor was needed, he would of course send for the best specialist – if necessary, all the way to Germany or England. However, to humour Olivia and Harry, he consented to send a car for Dr. Saunders.

Dr. Saunders, pleased and flattered to be called in by royalty, laid his finger-tips together and used many technical terms. He puffed while he spoke and with each word blew out the hairs of his moustache so that they fluttered around his mouth as if stirred by a breeze. The Nawab treated him with that exaggerated courtesy that Olivia had learned to recognise as his way of expressing contempt: but it made Dr. Saunders, who took it at face value, expand even further inside his tight shantung suit. The sight of the two of them seated opposite each other – the Nawab leaning forward deferentially while the doctor expounded and expanded – gave Harry the giggles and, seeing him, Olivia too could not stop. Dr. Saunders did not notice but the Nawab did and, glad to provide such good entertainment for his friends, he insisted that the doctor stay for luncheon.

Dr. Saunders reached new heights at the dining table. Flushed with enjoyment of his host's food and drink, he allowed himself to be prompted into expressing his considered opinion of India and Indians. He had many anecdotes to relate in illustration of his theme, mainly

4 **gaunt** [gɔːnt]: hager 5 **stray**: move away (without intending to) **neckline**: the edge of a dress at the neck 11 **consent**: permit, agree 17 **contempt**: Verachtung 18 **take sth. at face value**: believe that sth. is really what it appears to be **expand**: become bigger **shantung**: soft Chinese silk 20 **deferential**: ehrerbietig, respektvoll **expound sth.**: explain sth. by giving a lot of details 21 **give sb. the giggles**: make sb. laugh in a silly way 26–27 **be prompted**: veranlasst werden

drawn from his hospital experience. Although Olivia had heard most of them before, she shared Harry's amusement at the Nawab's way of eliciting them.

'Then what did you do, Doctor?'

'Then, Nawab Sahib, I had the fellow called to my office and, no further argument, smartly boxed his ears for him, one-two, one-two.'

'You did quite right, Doctor. Quite right. You set a good example.'

'It's the only way to deal with them, Nawab Sahib. It's no use arguing with them, they're not amenable to reason. They haven't got it here, you see, up here, the way we have.'

'Exactly, Doctor. You have hit the – what is it, Harry?'

'Nail on the head.'

'Quite right. The nail on the head.' The Nawab nodded gravely.

After a while Olivia ceased to be amused. Dr. Saunders was too blatantly stupid, the joke had gone on too long. Harry also became weary of it. With his usual sensitivity, the Nawab at once became aware of the change in atmosphere. He threw down his napkin and said 'Come, Olivia and Harry.' Leaving the doctor unceremoniously behind, he led the other two upstairs to Harry's suite. There he threw himself into a chair and, laying back his head, gave way to loud laughter. He was quite hurt when the other two did not join in: 'I have worked so hard and done so much only to amuse you two,' he complained.

'It's cruelty to animals.'

'But he calls *us* animals,' the Nawab pointed out.

Harry said 'He's just an old bore. Why ever did you bring him.'

'It was *she*,' the Nawab said, pointing at Olivia. But when she looked embarrassed, he tried to make it up to her: 'He is not a bore. He is very amusing. "We doctors at home in England",' he said, laying his fingertips together and blowing out an imaginary moustache. It was not a very good imitation, but to oblige him the other two laughed. At first he was gratified but then his mood changed and he said with disgust 'You are right. He is a bore. Tcha, why did we bring him, let's send him away.'

3 **elicit sth.**: etwas entlocken 6 **box sb.'s ears**: jdn. ohrfeigen 9 **amenable** [ə'mi:nəbl]: zugänglich 15 **blatant** ['bleɪtənt]: obvious 25 **bore** (n): person who is boring 30 **oblige sb.** (fml): do what sb. wants as a favour 30–31 **be gratified**: hoch erfreut sein 31 **disgust**: Abscheu

Olivia felt compelled to say: 'He really is exceptionally obnoxious. Don't judge by him.'

The Nawab looked at her rather coldly: 'Don't judge what by him?'

'All of us.'

'Who's us?' Harry asked her. He too sounded hostile. Olivia felt herself floundering – it was the same sensation she had had at the Crawford's dinner party, of not knowing where she stood.

'I don't know how you feel about it,' Harry pursued, 'but please don't lump me in with all that lot.'

'But, Harry, the Crawfords – for instance – they are not like Dr. Saunders, you know they're not. Or the Minnies. Or for that matter Douglas and –'

'You?'

'All are the same,' the Nawab said suddenly and decisively.

Olivia had a shock – did he mean her too? Was she included? She looked at his face and was frightened by the feelings she saw so plainly expressed there: and it seemed to her that she could not bear to be included in these feelings, that she would do anything *not* to be.

'I shall send him away,' the Nawab said, calling loudly for servants. He gave orders that Dr. Saunders was to be put in a car and despatched home. 'Oh and pay him, pay him', he said. '*You* do it. Just give him the money, he will take it', he told his servant and laughed; and the servant smiled too at this insult that was being delivered to Dr. Saunders of being paid off by servants.

'I'd better go too,' Olivia said, swallowing tears.

'You?' cried the Nawab. 'With him?' He sounded outraged. 'Do you think I would allow you to go home in the same car with *him*? Is that the idea you have of my hospitality? Of my friendship?' He seemed deeply hurt.

She protested 'But I have to go home soon – and since the car is going –' She was laughing, feeling suddenly terribly light-hearted.

1 **obnoxious**: offensive, unpleasant 5 **hostile**: feindselig 6 **flounder**: be unable to react because of confusion 9 **lump sb./sth. in with sb./sth. else**: consider sb./sth. to be the same as sb./sth else **lot** (n): a particular group of people 14 **decisive**: bestimmt 20 **despatch sb./sth.**: send sb./sth. to a destination 23 **insult**: Beleidigung

'Another car will go. Ten cars will go if necessary. Sit down please. Oh we are having a rotten time instead of enjoying ourselves, why are we like this? Harry! Olivia! Please be jolly! I will tell you a dream I had last night – you will laugh – it was about Mrs. Crawford. No but wait, wait – she was not Mrs. Crawford, she was an *hijra* and she was doing like this.' He clapped his hands as one dancing and laughed uproariously. 'She was with a whole troupe of them all singing and dancing, but I recognised her quite easily. It is true,' he said, 'she does look like an hijra.'

Olivia asked 'What is an *hijra*?'

The Nawab laughed again: 'I will show you.'

It was then that he called his attendant young men and ordered eunuchs to be brought to sing and dance. And for the rest of Olivia's stay that day she had a very enjoyable time.

* * * *

20 June. Shortly before the monsoon, the heat becomes very intense. It is said that the more intense it becomes the more abundantly it will draw down the rains, so one wants it to be as hot as can be. And by that time one has accepted it – not got used to but accepted; and moreover, too worn-out to fight against it, one submits and endures. There are compensations too. The hotter it is, the sweeter are the mangoes and the sugar melons, the more pungent the scent of the jasmine. The gul mohar tree, spreading its branches like a dancer, blooms with astonishing scarlet blossoms. All sorts of sweet sherbets are sold in the bazaar, and the glasses in which they are served (though perhaps not very clean) are packed to the top with crushed ice (also not very clean but who cares).

On Sunday Inder Lal and I went to Baba Firdaus' grove for a picnic. It was my idea though when we were sitting, soaked with perspiration, in the bus and rattling through the broiling landscape, I wondered

2 **rotten** (adj): bad 3 **jolly**: happy, cheerful 6 **uproarious**: very noisy with a lot of laughter 16 **abundant**: reichlich 19 **submit**: sich unterwerfen **endure**: suffer patiently 20 **compensation**: Ausgleich 21 **pungent** [ˈpʌndʒənt]: durchdringend **scent**: smell 21–22 **gul mohar tree**: tropical tree with red blossoms 23 **sherbet**: sweet fizzy drink 27 **soaked** (adj): durchnässt

whether it had been such a good one. We got off and toiled up the rocky, completely barren and exposed path that led to the grove: but once there, it was like being received in Paradise. The sun could not reach here through the foliage of the trees; the sound of the little spring trickled cool and fresh. Inder Lal lay down at once under a tree, but I was so delighted with the place that I wandered around it. The contrast could hardly have been more complete with the last time I had been here – on the Husband's Wedding Day – when it was packed with pilgrims and loudspeakers. Now it was quite, quite still except for the water and the birds, and sometimes the leaves rustled. I bathed my hands and face in the spring which was so shallow that I could touch the stone-cold pebbles in its bed. I inspected the shrine and found it to be a very plain structure with an arched entrance and a small striped dome like a sugar-melon set on top. Inside it was rather thickly whitewashed – probably each time a Husband's Wedding Day came round a new coat of paint was hurriedly slapped on; the latticed window was covered with red threads tied by supplicants. There was no tomb – Baba Firdaus' whereabouts at the time of his death were unknown – but a little whitewashed mound of stone stood in the centre. On this were draped several strings of flowers, most of them dead but one or two quite fresh. The place was so completely deserted, so full of silence and solitude, that I wondered who could have left them there.

When Inder Lal woke up, I unpacked the sandwiches I had brought for us. He had never had sandwiches before and ate them with interest, always glad to be learning something new. What was also new to him was to have an outing with only one other person present instead of the usual crowd of family and friends. He said he appreciated the conversation that could be had when there were only two people together, each then being in a position to disclose the contents of his heart to the other. I waited for him to do so, but he only asked me some rather banal

1 **toil**: move slowly and with difficulty 2 **exposed** (adj): not sheltered with trees, etc. 4 **foliage**: Blätter, Blätterwerk 10 **rustle**: rascheln 11 **spring**: Quelle 12 **pebble**: Kieselstein 17 **thread**: Faden **supplicant** (fml): person asking for sth., e.g. by praying to God 20 **drape sth.**: hang sth. loosely on sth. 29 **disclose sth.** (fml): make sth. known

questions, such as about picnics in England. He listened eagerly to my answers and kept trying to draw out further details. 'For my information only,' he said. It is a phrase he often uses when asking me questions. He seems to relish collecting irrelevant bits of information and to store them away for further use. His mother does the same with things. I have seen her reverently pick up and smoothe out a wrapper of chocolate paper I have thrown away, corks, empty bottles, shreds of cloth. She hoards them away in her big trunk and when I ask what for she is surprised. To her, as to him, every scrap is useful or could become so in the future.

He said 'Look what I have brought.'

He produced two pieces of red string; he said we had to tie them to the lattice in the shrine and then our wishes would be fulfilled. We took off our sandals and entered the shrine. He first tied his piece of string, to show me how to do it; he shut his eyes and wished fervently. I said 'I thought it was only for barren women.'

'All wishes are heard,' he said. 'Now you do it.' He handed me my string and watched me with interest: 'You can say your wish aloud,' he encouraged me. 'If you are alone or only one friend with you.'

Instead of answering, I pointed at the fresh garlands laid on the stone mound: 'Who do you think can have put them? It looks as if no one's been here for ages.'

He said 'Even if a place like this is in the middle of the desert, one thousand miles from anywhere, people will come … What did you wish?'

I smiled and went back to sit in our place under the tree; he followed me. 'Tell me,' he coaxed, really consumed with curiosity.

'Well what do you think?' But whatever it was, he felt embarrassed to say. So now I was curious, wondering what he could be thinking.

He parried: 'How can I say. I am not a magician or other person with powers to read another's thoughts. But if you tell me,' he said cunningly, 'I will tell you.'

4 **relish sth.**: enjoy sth. 6 **reverent**: ehrfürchtig **smoothe out sth.**: etwas glätten **wrapper**: Verpackung 7 **shred**: Schnipsel 8 **hoard sth.**: collect and store sth., often secretly and in large quantities 20 **garland**: circle of flowers, leaves, etc. 26 **coax sb.**: persuade sb. gently **consumed with**: full of 29 **parry**: abwehren 30 **cunning**: clever at deceiving people

'Let's try and guess.'

'You first.' He enjoyed this game.

I pretended to concentrate very hard while he looked at me eagerly. 'I think,' I said finally, 'it had something to do with your office.'

At once his face fell – in astonishment, in consternation: 'How did you know?'

'Oh I just guessed.'

But I wished I hadn't. He became depressed and no longer enjoyed the game. When I said 'Now it's your turn,' he gloomily shook his head. Sunk in his own troubles, he was no longer interested in my wishes.

But now I wanted him to be. I really had the desire – as he had said – to disclose the contents of my heart to another. However, it is difficult enough to do that to a person conversant with one's life and problems: what then to say to *him* to whom these are utterly unknown and alien! If I had had a definite wish – such as for a husband, a baby, or the removal of an enemy – I would have been glad to tell him. But in fact, while I had tied my thread with all the others, there had been nothing really definite I knew to wish for. Not that my life is so fulfilled that there is nothing left to ask; but, on the contrary, that it is too lacking in essentials for me to fill up the gaps with any one request.

However, at that moment I did have a desire, and a strong one: to get close to him. And since this seemed impossible to do with words, I laid my hand on his. Then he looked at me in an entirely different way. There was no lack of interest now! But it was difficult to tell *what* there was. I could feel his hand tremble under mine: and then I saw that his lips trembled too. Perhaps because he was about to speak; perhaps with desire, or with fear. There was certainly fear in his eyes as they looked at me. He did not know what to do next, nor what I was going to do next. I could see – it was ludicrous! – how everything he had heard about Western women rushed about in his head. And yet at the same time he was a healthy young man – his wife was away – we were alone in a romantic spot (getting more romantic every moment as the sun began to set). Although the next few moves were up to me, once I had made

5 **consternation**: feeling of great surprise or shock 9 **gloomy**: sad, without hope 13 **conversant** (fml): vertraut 15 **removal**: Beseitigung 29 **ludicrous**: ridiculous, absurd

them he was not slow to respond. Afterwards he made the same joke the Nawab had made, about what had happened here on the original Husband's Wedding Day to make the barren wife pregnant.

1923

One day Harry arrived with the car sent for Olivia. She was ready to leave at once but he said to wait awhile, he wanted to rest before going back. He sat on and on. He seemed ready to spend the day. She said, several times, 'If we don't leave soon, it'll get too hot.'

'Play something,' he said, indicating the piano. 'Go on, I haven't heard you in ages.'

'And then we'll go,' she bargained.

She sat down at the piano and began to play with her customary dash. She played Debussy, and Harry put back his head against the yellow armchair and shut his eyes and one foot tapped with pleasure. But after a while she played too fast and stumbled, and once or twice a key got stuck and she banged at it impatiently. She broke off: 'I'm out of practice. Come on now, Harry, we must go.'

'Why are you out of practice?'

'It's too hot to play. And have you *heard* the piano, what a state it's in?' She banged at a defective note again. 'This is simply no climate for a piano and that's all there is to it. Get up, Harry, do.'

'You could get a tuner. From Bombay.'

'It's not worth it. I hardly play now.'

'What a pity.'

He said this with such feeling that she became thoughtful. Why hadn't she been playing? She hadn't asked herself that before, had vaguely thought it was too hot or she just didn't feel like it. But there was something more, and she tried to think what that could be.

'Debussy,' she said. 'Schumann. It's so … unsuitable.' She laughed.

'It suits me,' Harry said.

'*Here*?'

11 **bargain**: verhandeln 13 **dash**: energy, confidence **Claude Debussy** (1862–1918): French composer who developed a style known as musical impressionism 15 **stumble**: einen Fehler machen 29 **unsuitable**: unpassend

'Why not?' He looked around her room and repeated 'Why not. You've made it very nice in here. Very nice indeed.' He settled deeper into his chair as if never wanting to leave again: 'The Oasis,' he said.

'Don't start that again please.' It really irritated her. 'I can't see why anyone should want an oasis. Why it should be necessary.'

'Goodness,' he said, 'how tough you are, Olivia, who'd have thought it ... And you're never ill either, are you.'

'Of course not. Why should I be.' She was quite scornful. 'That's all just psychological.'

'Last night I was so bad again. And I haven't eaten Indian food in weeks. I don't know what it's due to.'

'I told you: psychological.'

'You may be right. I'm certainly feeling quite psychological ... In fact I'm feeling,' he said, shutting his eyes again but this time in pain, 'as if I couldn't stand it another day.' And he sounded as if he really couldn't.

She tried to be sympathetic but could not overcome her impatience. For one thing, she was so impatient to be off! And he just sat there, not wanting to move. From the servant quarters came the sound of a voice chanting and a drum being beaten in accompaniment, both on one flat note and without pause in absolute monotony.

'It's like brain fever,' Harry said.

'What? ... Oh, that. I don't hear it any more. It's been going on for days. There's always something like that going on in the quarters. Someone dying or getting born or married. I think it may be why I don't play the piano much any more. I mean, it doesn't exactly harmonise, does it ... Harry, we must go or we'll die of heat on the road.'

'I don't want to go,' he said.

She had a moment of panic. Her voice trembled: 'What about the car?'

'We'll send it back.'

Olivia stared at the tips of her white shoes. She sat very still. Harry watched her but she pretended not to notice. At last he said: 'What's the matter with you, Olivia?' He spoke very gently. 'Why are you so eager to go?'

8 **scornful**: verächtlich, höhnisch 19 **accompaniment**: Begleitung

'We're expected.' Hearing how lame that sounded, she became more irritated with him: 'And you don't think I *like* sitting around here all day, day after day, staring at the wall and waiting for Douglas to come home, do you? I can well see how people can go batty that way … like Mrs. Saunders. Just sitting inside the house and imagining things. I don't want to become like Mrs. Saunders. But if I go on sitting here by myself, I shall.'

'Is that why you like to come to the Palace?'

'Douglas knows I go to the Palace. He knew about Dr. Saunders coming there – he spoke to him himself – and that I'd been to see you.'

'Yes to see *me*.'

This hung on the air and did not cease to do so after she replied 'You're jealous, Harry, that's what it is. Yes you are!' She laughed. 'You want to be the *only* one – I mean,' she said, 'in the Palace, the only guest there.' She said this last bit quickly but not quickly enough. She was blushing now and felt entangled.

'All right,' he said. 'We'll go.'

He got up and moved to the door, putting on his solar topee. She felt that now – out of pride, or to prove her innocence – she ought to be the one to hang back. She hesitated for a moment but found that she did not, after all, have enough pride (or innocence) for that. She followed him quite quickly to the car.

That journey was uncomfortable, and not only because of heat and dust. They hardly spoke as if angry with each other. Yet Olivia was not angry, and once or twice she did try to talk to him but what came out might as well have been left unsaid. She could not bring herself to speak about what was disturbing her – she was afraid that, if she did, she might say more than she meant; or he might misinterpret whatever it was she did mean.

Suddenly Harry said 'There he is.'

A red open sports car was parked across the road. As they approached, the Nawab, wearing a checked cap and motorist's goggles, stood up in it and made traffic policeman gestures. They stopped, he said 'Where have you been? I have been waiting and waiting.'

1 **lame**: lahm   4 **batty** (infml): crazy, mad   16 **entangled** (adj) ertappt, verwickelt
32 **checked**: kariert   **goggles** (pl): Rennbrille

He had come to meet them because he wanted to go to Baba Firdaus' shrine. He was tired of being shut up in the Palace, he said. He invited them to climb into his sports car which he was driving himself. When Harry said he didn't feel like it, he wanted to go home, the Nawab wasted no more time on him but said 'You come, Olivia.'

She too wasted no time on Harry but got in beside the Nawab. They drove away in one direction while the chauffeur drove Harry in the other. He could be seen sitting alone at the back of the limousine, looking pale and cross.

'Why is he so cross?' the Nawab asked Olivia. 'Do you think he is ill? Is he ill? Has he said anything to you?'

He was deeply concerned and continued, for most of the way, to talk about Harry. He said he knew Harry was often homesick and wanted to go back to England to see his mother; and the Nawab wanted him to go but at the same time – 'Olivia, can you understand this, does it sound very selfish' – he could not bring himself to part with him. 'I can see you think I am very selfish,' he concluded sadly.

She knew it was not necessary to contradict. Her role was to listen and she was content with that; also to be next to him and sometimes to steal a look at him where he sat dressed up in cap and goggles and steering his car.

'Often I have wanted to say to him: "Harry, your Mother wants you at home, you also want to be with her: go." Sometimes I *have* said. Once everything was done, his berth booked, his baggage packed. At the last moment I broke down. I could not tolerate this parting. Then it was he who said "no I shall stay" … Now we have to get out and walk, will it be too hot for you, Olivia?'

He led the way up the rocky path to Baba Firdaus' grove. He went on talking and she listened to him and so did not much feel the sun beating down.

He said 'There are certain people who if they are absent life becomes hard to bear. Once I asked a faqir from Ajmere (a very holy person): "Why *these* people? Why they and not others?" He gave me the following reply which I like very much: "These are the people who once sat close to you in Paradise:" It is a beautiful idea, isn't it, Olivia? That we sat close to each other once in Paradise.'

They had arrived in the grove. He parted the branches for her, they entered. But just as they did so, some men emerged from the shrine. Olivia had a shock. They were rough and armed and for a moment they stared dangerously at the Nawab and Olivia. But next moment, realising who it was, they fell at the Nawab's feet.

He told Olivia to sit under a tree. She watched him talk to the men. He was easy and familiar with them. They stood before him in an attitude of humility and with a look of adoration on their desperado faces. She was quite sure they were desperadoes. She studied them – they looked like mediaeval bandits – but not once did they dare glance in her direction. The Nawab dismissed them quite soon, then called her into the shrine.

'Look what I have brought,' he said.

He held two lengths of red string. She tied hers first, then he tied his. Afterwards he asked 'What did you wish?'

'Is one supposed to tell?'

'If there is only one person there with you … You know what women come here for? What they wish? Is that what you wished also?'

'Yes,' she said.

'Ah'.

There was a silence; then he said: 'It is all superstition. But perhaps it is true. It may be true; there are many stories of miracles that have happened. You have heard the story of the Husband's Wedding Day? Of course it is all quite unscientific, and educated people like you and I –'

'Still we did tie strings.'

'Only for fun.'

'Who were those men?'

He didn't answer at once, and when he did, it was with another question: 'Who do you think they were?' He gave her one of his shrewd looks, then laughed: 'I suppose you think they are bad men. You must have heard many stories I think, isn't it, and you believe they are true.' Again she felt she did not have to defend herself or answer him.

'But if they are bad men,' he went on, 'I think they can't be so very bad because look what they have come here for.' He pointed to the mound in the shrine on which some fresh garlands had just been laid

29 **shrewd**: schlau

and sticks of incense were still smouldering. 'You see, they did not come for any bad purpose but to pay their devotions.'

He looked at her as if testing her reaction. But she had no reaction, only some very strong physical sensations. The vast simmering plain of heat surrounding the grove trickled here and there through the leaves. The Nawab's overwhelming presence was concentrated now on her alone.

'Come,' he said. 'Sit with me.'

Both sat on the step leading into the shrine. He spoke to her in a gentle, reasoning voice: 'Yes perhaps they are outlaws, it is true, but still they are human beings who come here – you see – to pray and tell their wishes. Like you and I also.' He was silent for a while, as if to let her feel the truth of his words; or perhaps the communion between himself and her, to let that sink in.

'When we go from here, Olivia, will you go back to Satipur and say yes, the Nawab is a bad person, now I have seen with my own eyes that he meets with outlaws, dacoits – he is hand in glove with them. You will go back and say that, Olivia?'

Now he was really waiting for an answer, and she did not hesitate to give him one. 'Do you really believe I'd do that,' she said with such sincerity – indeed, indignation – that he was satisfied with her. He respectfully touched her arm with his finger-tips.

'No I don't believe,' he said. 'And this is why I open my heart to you and tell you everything … Don't think please that I want you to say only he is a very good person, a fine and noble soul. Not at all. Of course I would like to be a fine and noble soul – it is necessary for all of us to strive for this – but also I know how far I am from such a goal. Yes very far indeed,' he said and looked discouraged.

'Who isn't,' Olivia said. He touched her arm in the same way as before, and partly she wished he wouldn't and partly she longed for him to do it again.

1 **smoulder**: burn slowly without a flame 2 **devotions** (pl): prayers or other religious worship 4 **vast**: huge **simmering**: brütend **plain**: Ebene 5 **trickle**: flow slowly, spread slowly 14 **sink in**: (of words or an event) be fully understood 17 **be hand in glove with sb.**: work together closely with sb. 21 **indignation**: Empörung 27 **strive for sth.**: nach etwas streben

'You are right. We are all far from it. But there are some people – many people,' he said, pausing to let her think who they were: 'They make themselves into judges over others, saying this is good, this bad, as if they are all-knowing. Who is Major Minnies that he should say to me don't do this, and don't do that, who has given him the right to say this to me? To *me*!' he said, incredulously pointing at himself. 'To the Nawab Sahib of Khatm.' He was speechless for a moment.

'Do you know how we got our title? It was in 1817. My ancestor, Amanullah Khan, had been fighting for many, many years. Sometimes he fought the Mahrattas, sometimes the Rajputs or the Moghuls or the British. Those were very disturbed times. He went from place to place with his men, wherever there was fighting and booty to be picked up. They had to live, all of them! Sometimes, when he did not have the wherewithal to pay his soldiers, they mutinied against him and then he had to flee not from the enemy but from his own men, can you imagine! But when things picked up for him again, they all came back and others also joined him. So sometimes he was very up and sometimes quite down. Such was his life. Olivia: I envy him. His name was feared by everyone – including the British! When they saw they could not subdue him by any means, then they wanted him for their ally. Oh they were always very cunning people and knew which way to take out their own advantage. They offered him the lands and revenues of Khatm and also the title of Nawab. And because he was tired at that time, he said yes all right and he became a Nawab and sat down here. Because he was tired.' He became gloomy. 'But I think you can get tired also sitting in a palace. Then you feel it would be better not to have anything but to fight your enemies and kill them. You feel you would like to do that very much. Don't you think, Olivia, it is better to meet your enemies in this way than to have them secretly plotting against you and whispering slanders? I think it is very much better!' he cried, suddenly very upset.

She put out her hand and laid it on his chest as if to soothe him. And really he was soothed; he said 'How kind you are to me.' He laid his

6 **incredulous**: not willing to believe 12 **booty**: goods that are stolen during wars, etc. 14 **wherewithal**: the money needed for sth. 19 **subdue sb.**: bring sb. under control by force 22 **revenue**: (Staats)einkünfte 29 **plot against sb.**: sich gegen jdn. verschwören **slander**: Verleumdung 32 **soothe sb.**: calm or comfort sb.

hand on top of hers and pressed it closer against his chest. She felt drawn to him by a strength, a magnetism that she had never yet in all her life experienced with anyone.

'Listen,' he said. 'Once it happened that a Marwar prince did something to displease him. I think he did not offer opium out of the correct silver chalice – it was only a very small thing, but Amanullah Khan was not the man to sit quiet when insulted. Not like me.' When she began to protest, he said 'I have to, what can I do. I am helpless ... He invited this Marwar prince and all his retainers to a feast. A ceremonial tent was put up and all preparations made and the guests came ready to eat and drink. Amanullah Khan greeted his enemy at the door of the tent and folded him to his heart. But when they were all inside, he gave a secret sign and his men cut the ropes of the tent and the Marwar prince and all his party were entangled within the canvas. When they were trapped there like animals, Amanullah Khan and his men took their daggers and stabbed with them through the canvas again and again till there was not one enemy left alive. We still have that tent and the blood is so fresh and new, Olivia, it is as if it had happened yesterday.' He must have felt that she was trying to remove her hand from his heart so he held it against himself tighter. She could not escape him now, even if she had wanted to.

'Not here,' he said. He led her away from the shrine and they lay together under a tree. Afterwards he made a joke: 'It is the secret of the Husband's Wedding Day,' he said.

'Then what did you make me tie the string for?' she asked.

He laughed and laughed, well pleased with her.

* * * *

31 July. Maji has informed me that I am pregnant. At first I didn't believe her – how could anyone possibly tell so early, even if it were true – but she was absolutely certain. Moreover, she has warned me that I had better be careful because soon all the midwives in town would come to

4 **Marwar**: region in Rajasthan (western India) 6 **chalice**: Kelch 9 **retainer** (old use): servant **feast**: a large meal 12 **fold sb. to your heart**: (here) hold sb. closely, embrace sb. closely 14 **entangled** (adj): verheddert

me to offer their services. They always know, she said, long before anyone else does. They can tell by the way a woman walks and holds herself. That is their business and they are always on the look-out for custom. There is no doubt, she said, that soon they would get on to me.

She was so positive that I have begun to believe her. I assumed that she knew by some kind of second sight – it always seems to me that she has powers that others don't. Once I had a headache and she put her hand on my forehead and I can't describe the strange sensations transmitted to me. They lasted for days. So I thought that nothing about Maji would ever surprise me – until she told me, quite casually, that she knew about me because she herself had been a midwife. That surprised me more than if she actually had revealed supernatural powers.

She laughed at my reaction. She said what did I think, that she had always led this idle life of hers? Not at all. She had been a married woman and had had several children. Unfortunately her husband had not been much of a breadwinner – he had preferred his toddy and the company of friends gathered around the toddy shop – so the burden of looking after the family had fallen on her. Her mother had been a midwife and so had her grandmother and both had taught her all they knew. (I wondered about her mother and grandmother – they might have been the women who had attended Olivia! It was possible.) But after her husband died and her children were settled, she gave up her profession and spent several years going to holy places to pick up whatever instruction she could. Finally she had come back here to Satipur and built herself this little hut to live in. Her friends have been looking after her ever since, bringing her what food she needs so she doesn't have a care in the world. Her children all live rather far away, but sometimes one or other of them comes to visit her or writes her a letter.

I was so surprised to hear all this – having never thought of her as having had a worldly life – that I quite forgot what she had told me about myself. It was she who reminded me; she laid her hand on my

6 **second sight**: the ability to see into the future 8–9 **transmit sth.**: etwas übertragen 12 **reveal sth.**: etwas offenbaren 14 **idle** ['aɪdəl]: lazy, not working hard 16 **breadwinner**: the person who earns money in order to support the family **toddy**: sweet alcoholic drink 17 **burden**: Last 19 **midwife**: Hebamme

abdomen and asked me what I intended to do. She said she would help me if I wanted help – I didn't understand her at first, and it was only when she repeated it that I realised she was offering me an abortion. She said I could trust her completely, for although it is many years since she has practised professionally, she still knows all there is to know about these matters. There are several ways to procure an abortion and she has at one time or other performed all of them. It is a necessary part of an Indian midwife's qualifications because in many cases it is the only way to save people from dishonour and suffering. She told me of various abortions she has performed in this good cause, and I was so fascinated that again I forgot all about my own case. But later, on the way home in the rain – the monsoon has started – I did think about it. Then my sensations were mainly of amusement and interest, so that I went skipping in and out of puddles, laughing to myself when I trod in them and got splashed.

15 August. Chid has come back. He is so changed that at first I could not recognise him. He no longer wears his orange robe but has acquired a pair of khaki pants and a shirt and a pair of shoes. Beads and begging bowl have also gone and his shaved hair is beginning to grow back in tiny bristles. From a Hindu ascetic he has become what I can only describe as a Christian boy. The transformation is more than outward. He has become very quiet – not only does he not talk in his former strain but he hardly talks at all. And he is ill again.

Apart from trips to the bathroom, he is mostly asleep in a corner of my room. He hasn't told me anything about how or why he parted company with Inder Lal's mother and Ritu. Nor do I have any idea what happened to him to change him this way. He doesn't want to talk about it. The most he will say is 'I can't stand the smell' (Well of course I know what he means – the smell of people who live and eat differently from oneself; I used to notice it even in London when I was near Indians in crowded buses or tubes). Chid can't bear Indian food any more. He will only accept plain boiled food, and what he likes best is when I make

1 **abdomen**: belly 3 **abortion**: Abtreibung 6 **procure sth.**: achieve sth. 14 **skip**: hüpfen **puddle**: Pfütze 20 **bristles** (pl): Stoppeln 23 **strain** (fml): way of speaking

him an English soup. The smell of Indian cooking makes him literally cry out with nausea and disgust.

Inder Lal is very disappointed in him. He keeps waiting for the fireworks of high-flown Hindu doctrine to start again, but there is nothing like that left in Chid. In any case Inder Lal is not pleased with Chid's return. I ought to explain that, after our picnic at Baba Firdaus' shrine, there has been a change in my relationship with Inder Lal. He now comes up to my room at night. For the sake of the neighbours, he makes a pretence of going to sleep downstairs but when it is dark he comes creeping up. I'm sure everyone knows, but it doesn't matter. They don't mind. They realise that he is lonely and misses his family very much; no human being is meant to live without a family.

After Chid moved back in again, Inder Lal at first felt shy about his nightly visits. But I have assured him that it is all right because Chid is mostly sleeping. He just lies there and groans and it is difficult to believe that it is the same person who performed all those tremendous feats on me. Inder Lal and I lie on my bedding on the opposite side, and it is more and more delightful to be with him. He trusts me now completely and has become very affectionate. I think he prefers to be with me when it is dark. Then everything is hidden and private between us two alone. Also I feel it makes a difference that he cannot *see* me, for I'm aware that my appearance has always been a stumbling block to him. In the dark he can forget this and he also needn't feel ashamed of me before others. He can let himself go completely, and he does. I don't mean only physically (though that too) but everything there is in him – all his affection and playfulness. At such times I'm reminded of all those stories that are told of the child Krishna and the many pranks and high-spirited tricks he got up to. I also think of my pregnancy and I think of it as part of him.

But I have not told him about it.

I have *tried* to tell him. I specially went to call for him at his office and took him across the road to the British graveyard, that being the most secluded spot I could think of. It is not a place he is at all interested in; in fact, he had never even bothered to go into it before. The only

2 **nausea**: Übelkeit 16 **feat**: achievement, action 22 **stumbling block**: Hindernis 27 **prank** (infml): Streich 33 **secluded** (adj): (here) private

thing to make any impression on him was the Saunders' Italian angel which can still be seen rearing above the other graves: no longer in benign benediction but as a headless, wingless torso. Inder Lal did not seem put out by this mutilation. Probably it seemed natural to him – after all, he has grown up among armless Apsaras and headless Sivas riding on what is left of their bulls. In its present condition indeed the angel no longer looks Italian but quite Indian.

I showed him Lt. Edwards'grave and read out the inscription: '"*Kind and indulgent Father but most conspicuous* . . . " It means,' I told Inder Lal, looking round at him, 'he was a very good husband and father. Like you.'

'What can I do?' was his odd reply.

I think what he was saying was that he has no alternative but to be a good husband and father: having been thrown into that stage of life, whether he likes it or not. And on the whole I think he doesn't. Anyway, I have decided not to tell him about my pregnancy. I don't want to spoil anything.

1923

When Olivia found that she was pregnant, she didn't tell Douglas. She put it off from day to day, and in the end it happened that she told the Nawab first.

One morning, on arrival in the Palace, she found everyone running around carrying and packing and giving each other conflicting instructions. Even Harry was packing up in his room and seemed in rather a good mood. He said they were going to Mussoorie at last, the Begum had decided the night before. One of her ladies had been indisposed and had been advised a change of air, so the Begum said they would all go. It would do Harry good too, she thought; she had been very worried about him.

'Oh?' said Olivia. 'Do you see her often?'

3 **benign benediction** [bɪˈnaɪn]: freundliche Segnung 4 **mutilation**: Verstümmelung 5 **apsara**: (in Hinduism and Buddhism) female angel 16 **spoil sth.**: etwas verderben 27 **indisposed** (fml): not very well

Ever since the day Harry had pointed out that not being received in the purdah quarters was a discourtesy to Olivia, they had not mentioned the Begum. But Olivia was aware that Harry was received there on a footing of intimacy.

'Every day,' he said. 'We play cards, she likes it.' He changed the subject: 'And the Nawab also says he is bored being here, so today everyone is packing.'

'He's bored?'

'So he says. But there's something else too.' He frowned and went on packing very meticulously.

'What?'

'Oh I don't know Olivia.' Although reluctant to talk, he did seem to want to share his feelings. 'He won't tell me exactly but I know there's some trouble. As a matter of fact, Major Minnies is with him right now. Didn't you see his car outside? I was wondering about that, hoping you wouldn't collide on the stairs or something.'

'Why not? What's it matter? I've come to see you.'

'Quite.' He went on packing.

She interrupted him impatiently: 'Do stop that now, Harry, and tell me what's going on. I ought to know.' He turned around then from where he was kneeling on the floor and gave her a look that made her emend to 'I'd like to know.'

'So would I,' Harry said. He left his suitcase and came to sit near her. 'Or would I. Sometimes I feel I'd just as soon not.'

They were silent. Both looked out of the latticed window framing the garden below. The water channels intersecting the lawns reflected a sky that shifted and sailed with monsoon clouds.

Harry said 'I know he's in all sorts of trouble. It's been going on for years. Financial troubles – Khatm is bankrupt – and then all that business with Sandy and the Cabobpurs who've been complaining right and left and trying to bring a case about her dowry. And of course that makes him more stubborn to fight back though he can't really afford to.

4 **footing** (n): basis 9 **frown**: die Stirn runzeln 10 **meticulous**: very accurate
22 **emend sth.**: correct sth. 26 **intersect**: divide into sections

Simla has been getting very acrimonious lately, and I know he's had some rather difficult interviews with Major Minnies. I *hate* it when Major Minnies comes here.' He flushed and seemed reluctant to continue; but he did: 'Because afterwards he's always so upset. You'll see now when he comes up. He usually takes it out on me – don't think I'm complaining, I'm not, I'm glad if that makes him feel better. Because I can see how hurt he is. He's terribly terribly sensitive, Olivia, and of course being talked to like that by Major Minnies – being threatened –'

'How dare they!' cried Olivia.

'You see, the truth is he's only a very little prince and they don't have to be all that careful with him the way they'd have to be for instance with the Cabobpur family. And he feels it terribly. He knows what he is compared with the others. You should see old Cabobpur: he's just a gross swine, there's nothing royal about him. Whereas of course *he* is – '

'Yes.'

They heard his voice, his unmistakable step on the stairs. Both waited. He burst in without knocking – which was unusual: at other times he showed the most courteous diffidence in entering his guest's suite. But now of course he was greatly upset. He strode in and went straight to the window and sat there, smouldering.

He said 'I shall see the Viceroy himself. There is no point in talking with Major Minnies or anyone like that. It is like talking with – servants. I do not talk with servants.' His nostrils flared. 'Next time he comes here I shall refuse to see him. And I shall tear up any letters he dares to write to me and send the pieces back to him.' He turned on Harry: '*You* can take them back to him. You can fling them in his face and say here is your answer. But I suppose you would not like to do it.' He turned his fierce gaze on Harry who looked down. Olivia also did not like to look at the Nawab just then.

1 **Simla**: the British colonial government (which was based in Simla during the summer) **acrimonious**: bitter and angry 5 **take it out on sb.**: etwas an jdm. auslassen 14 **gross** [grəʊs] (infml): disgusting 18 **courteous diffidence**: höfliche Zurückhaltung 19 **stride (strode – stridden)**: move with long steps
20 **smouldering** (adj): glühend vor Zorn 21 **the Viceroy**: the British monarch's representative and highest British official in India 23 **flare**: sich aufblähen
28 **gaze**: strong long look

'I suppose you are afraid to do it. You are afraid of Major Minnies and other creatures of that nature. Answer! Don't sit there like a dumb stone, answer! Oh both of you are the same, you and Major Minnies. I don't know why you stay here with me. You want to be with him and other English people. You feel only for them, nothing for me at all.'

'You know that's not true.' Harry did his best to sound calm, reasonable.

It only infuriated the Nawab the more. He turned to Olivia: 'Now he is playing the Englishman with me. So cool and quiet and never losing his temper. He is playing Major Minnies with me. How different from these terrible orientals. Olivia, do you also hate and despise orientals? Of course you do. And you are right I think. Because we are very stupid people with feelings that we let others trample on and hurt to their heart's content. English people are so lucky – they have no feelings at all. Look at him,' he said, pointing at Harry. 'He has been with me so many years but what does he care for me? You see, he does not even try to answer me.' He sat by the window; his profile was outlined against gardens and sky, like the portrait of a ruler painted against the background of his own dominions. 'And you,' he said to Olivia. 'You also care nothing for me.'

'No? Then why am I here?'

'You have come to visit Harry. You want to be with him. And I'm very grateful to you that you are so nice to him because without you he would be most bored and lonely here. His health also is not good.' He got up and came over to Harry and touched his shoulder with affection.

Harry said 'I can't bear this.'

'I know you can't. I'm an unbearable person. Major Minnies is right.'

'That's not what I meant.'

'But it is true.'

He went out and Olivia followed him. As he walked down the stairs, she called his name which she had never used before. He stood still and looked up at her in surprise.

8 **infuriate sb.**: make sb. furious/angry 11 **oriental** (n): person from the East (e.g. India) **despise sb.**: jdn. verachten 13–14 **to your heart's content**: wie es einem gefällt 19 **dominion**: land held by a ruler or a king 25 **affection**: tenderness

She went running towards him, and as they met on the stairs, she was not at all sure what she was going to say. Afterwards, thinking about it, it seemed to her that she had not intended to tell him about her pregnancy. But that is what she did. She had to tell him in a low voice and he could not react much as they were in the middle of the Palace with servants and followers on every landing and who knew what ladies lurking behind curtains.

After that it wouldn't have been fair not to tell Douglas as well, and she did so that same night.

Next day she was waiting for Douglas, and also for Major Minnies whom they had invited to dine; but at about eight o'clock Douglas sent a peon from the office to say they would both be late. Something had happened again though he did not say what. Olivia sat waiting on the verandah. She had been waiting all day – not for Douglas but for a message from the Palace. None came. She did not know what had happened: they were supposed to have left for Mussoorie, but she could not believe that they would do so without seeing or communicating with her in some way first. She made up her mind that, if they had left, she would go too. She would tell Douglas that she could not stand the heat and must leave for the mountains immediately. Sitting there, alone and waiting in vain, she realised that it would not be possible for her to stay.

But when Douglas and their guest at last came, she did her best to overcome her disturbed state of mind and play the role expected of her. She sat at the dining table between white candles – her dress was white too, white lace – and chatted to them about a champagne party on the Cam she and Marcia had once attended where one of the boats had overturned. All the time she felt the two men to be as tense and disturbed as herself. When she left them to their brandy and cigars, she could hear them speaking together in worried tones; and when they came to join her on the front verandah, both were grave. She pleaded 'Won't you tell me what happened?'

They did so reluctantly (Major Minnies said it was a pity to spoil their mood). Of course the Nawab was involved again. His gang of

6 **landing** (n): floor 7 **lurk**: lauern 21 **in vain**: vergeblich 25 **lace**: Spitze
26 **Cam**: river running through Cambridge

dacoits, instead of confining themselves to the territories around Khatm, had strayed into the province under Mr. Crawford's jurisdiction. They had raided a village some five miles out of Satipur and had got away with cash and jewellery. No one had been killed but several villagers, who had tried to conceal their valuables, had been roughly handled. One woman had had her nose cut off. As soon as the villagers' report reached Satipur, Mr. Crawford and Douglas had informed Major Minnies who had at once driven over to the Palace. The Nawab had refused to receive him.

Olivia said 'But they've gone to Mussoorie.' She added carefully 'Harry told me. I saw him yesterday.'

'They were to have gone but the usual thing happened: the Begum changed her mind,' Major Minnies said. 'I don't know what it was this time – I think someone heard an owl which is of course very inauspicious before a journey – so they all had to unpack again.'

Olivia laughed – ostensibly at the superstition. She was gay with relief; they were still there, they had not left.

Major Minnies said 'I wasn't altogether surprised when he wouldn't see me: because unfortunately we had had rather a lively scene just yesterday. He got … quite excited.'

'Dashed impudence,' Douglas said with heat. 'I hope Simla isn't going to dilly-dally any further with him.'

'No it rather looks as if they won't. The wheels of Simla grind slowly but they grind exceedingly small. I'm afraid it was putting my case to him in these terms that got him so worked up.'

'Did that surprise you?' Olivia asked.

She felt Major Minnies look at her across the dark verandah. His cigar glowed as he pulled at it. He answered her calmly: 'No.'

It was Douglas who was not calm: 'It's time he was taught a lesson.'

'You talk as if he's a schoolboy!' cried Olivia.

2 **stray into sth.**: go to sth. where you should not be **jurisdiction**: Zuständigkeitsbereich 3 **raid sth.**: etwas überfallen 5 **conceal sth.**: hide sth. **valuables** (pl): Wertsachen 14 **inauspicious**: not a very good omen 16 **ostensibly** (adv): apparently 21 **dashed impudence**: bodenlose Frechheit 22 **dilly-dally**: waste time 23 **grind** [graɪnd]: mahlen

Major Minnies, fair and judicious, seemed to be intervening between them. 'In some ways,' he said, 'he is a fine man. He has some fine qualities – and if only these were combined with a little self-restraint, self-discipline …' Again Olivia felt his eyes on her in the dark; he said 'But somehow I admire him. And I think you do too.'

She said 'Yes.'

He nodded. 'You're right. No,' he said, as Douglas began to protest, 'we must be fair. He is a strong, forceful character, and perhaps given other circumstances – I've thought about him a great deal,' he said and now seemed to be addressing only Olivia. 'As you know, I've had dealings with him over several years and we have, I can't deny, had a lot of trouble with him.'

'And of what sort!' said Douglas, unable to hold back. 'He is a menace to himself, to us, and to the wretched inhabitants of his wretched little state. The worst type of ruler – the worst type of Indian – you can have.'

'Perhaps you're right; no doubt you're right' said Major Minnies. He was silent and thoughtful for a long time; at last he said, slowly, as one making a confession: 'Sometimes I feel that I'm not quite the right kind of person to be in India. Mary and I have spoken about it. Not that I would, at any stage of my career, have contemplated changing my job, this place – never, not for anything!' he said with an access of passion that surprised Olivia. 'But I do realise that in many ways I step over too far.'

'Into what?' asked Olivia.

'The other dimension.' He smiled, perhaps not wanting to sound too serious. 'I think I've allowed myself to get too fascinated. Take the Nawab: I can't deny that he does fascinate me – as I'm sure,' he told Olivia, 'he does you.'

'Oh gosh darling,' Douglas laughed, 'does he?'

'Well,' said Olivia, laughing back, 'he is a fascinating man … And terrifically handsome.'

1 **judicious**: reasonable 3 **self-restraint**: self-control 13 **menace**: threat 14 **wretched** (adj): miserable, pitiful 21 **contemplate sth.**: think about sth. for a long time 22 **access** (old use): sudden outburst

'Really?' Douglas asked, as if he had never seen him in that light.

'Oh absolutely,' said the Major. 'He is – a prince. No other word for him. The trouble is that his state is unfortunately not quite princely enough to satisfy either his ambition or indeed his need for money.'

Douglas was amused: 'So he has to take to armed robbery to make up for it?'

'I also think he's tremendously bored,' the Major said. 'He's a man who needs action – a large arena … I can always tell when he's feeling particularly frustrated because then he starts talking about his ancestor, Amanullah Khan.'

'That brigand,' said Douglas.

'Was he?' Olivia asked the Major.

'An adventurer – at a time of adventurers. That's what our Friend wants: adventure. He is not really the type to sit in a palace all day, or he would like not to be. But that's all there is for him, and moreover all he's ever known.'

'All he can do,' Douglas said.

'I used to know his father,' the Major told Olivia. 'What a character. A great penchant for the nautch girls – till he went to Europe and discovered chorus girls. He brought several back with him, and one of them stayed for years. She was in that room where he is now, what's his name.'

'Harry?'

'As a matter of fact, the old Nawab died in there. He had a stroke while he was with her … He was a great connoisseur of Urdu poetry. Every year there was a symposium at Khatm to which all the best poets came from all over India. The old Nawab wasn't a bad poet himself – he was always making up couplets – wait, let me see if I remember …'

After a moment he began to recite in mellifluous Urdu: it sounded very beautiful. Olivia looked up at the sky, furrowed with wavelets of

11 **brigand** (old use): bandit 19 **penchant**: Schwäche **nautch girl**: Indian dancing-girl 20 **chorus girl**: girl dancing in a group that plays a supporting part in a show or film 25 **connoisseur**: Kenner/in 28 **couplet**: two lines of poetry 29 **mellifluous**: lovely flowing 30 **furrowed**: zerfurcht **wavelet**: small wave

monsoon clouds, and the moon slowly sailing there. She followed her own thoughts.

'Are these dew drops on the rose or are they tears? Moon, your silver light turns all to pearls,' the Major translated. He apologised: 'Doesn't sound like much in English, I'm afraid.'

'No it never does,' Douglas agreed. In the dark he took Olivia's hand and held it in his own. The Major went on reciting in Urdu. His voice was loud and sonorous, and under cover of it Douglas whispered to his wife 'Are you all right?' She smiled at him and he pressed her hand. 'Happy?' he asked, and when she smiled again, he lifted her hand to his lips. The Major didn't see, he was looking up at the sky and reciting in Urdu; his voice was full of emotion – a sort of mixture of reverence and nostalgia. And afterwards he sighed: 'It gets you,' he said. 'It really does.'

'Doesn't it,' Olivia agreed politely. But she did not feel moved, either by the poetry or by his emotion. They did not, she felt, add up to much. She remembered what he had said – about going over too far – and it made her scornful. What did he know about that? If he thought that the nostalgic feelings engendered by a little poetry recited on a moonlit night was going too far! She laughed out loud at his presumption, and Douglas thought it was with happiness which made him very happy too.

'Did you know that the old Nawab died in this room?' Olivia asked Harry.

Harry said 'What else do you know?'

'Oh there was some chorus girl . . .'

He burst out laughing, then told her the rest of the story. After the old Nawab's death, the Begum had not permitted the girl to leave the Palace without first surrendering all the valuables the Nawab had given her. The girl – a tough little character from Yorkshire, Harry said – had tried to hold on to some of them, but there she had reckoned without the Begum. One day – actually, Harry said, it was the middle of the

3 **dew**: Tau 8 **sonorous**: volltönend 12 **reverence**: honour or respect that is felt or shown 19 **engender sth.** (fml): cause sth., produce sth. 20 **presumption**: Annahme, Vermutung 29 **surrender sth.**: etwas übergeben 31 **reckon without sb.**: nicht mit jdm. rechnen

night – the girl had turned up in Satipur with nothing but the clothes she stood up in (which happened to be a satin nightie and a Japanese kimono). She had been in a terrible state and claimed that the Begum had tried to poison her. The Collector and his wife, not entirely sceptical of her story, had done their best to calm her, promising to send her to Bombay and arrange for her to leave on the next boat home. But when they offered to send to the Palace for her clothes and other possessions, she became hysterical and begged them not to. She told them some tale she had heard about poisoned wedding garments that had been sent to an unwanted bride in the family: no sooner had the unfortunate victim put on the cloth-of-gold bodice than it clung to her, penetrating her with its deadly ointments. The girl swore that she knew this to be actual fact because the old Nawab himself had told her; also that all attempts to save the bride had been in vain and she had died writhing in agony. The old woman responsible for preparing the fatal garment was still alive and living in the Palace at Khatm. She lived a very pampered life in the purdah quarters where she was kept to pass on her art to others. 'Oh you don't know what goes on in there,' the girl said with a shudder. No one could talk her out of her fears, and although the Begum had of her own accord sent her suitcases after her, the girl refused to touch them but had left for Bombay wearing an odd assortment of clothes lent to her by the English ladies of Satipur.

Olivia smiled when she heard this story: 'She must have been crazy. Those poor old things in the purdah quarters.' She asked, casually, 'Do they know about me?'

'Know what about you?' Harry answered.

Olivia hardly ever thought about the purdah ladies. Sometimes it seemed to her that the curtains up in the galleries were moving, but she did not look up. The Nawab never spoke to her about his mother. Olivia realised that the Begum belonged to a different part of his life, perhaps to a more inner chamber of his heart: and this made Olivia proud and

11 **bodice**: woman's underclothes 12 **ointment**: Salbe 14 **writhe**: twist from pain **agony**: extreme physical or mental pain 16 **pamper sb.**: treat sb. with extreme or excessive care and attention 24 **casual**: beiläufig

stubborn so that she did not want to speak to him about his mother, or to acknowledge her existence.

But she found the Nawab more tender towards her than she had ever known him. He sent for her every day and made no secret in the Palace of the relations between them. He even began to take her into his own bedroom where she had not been before. She followed him wherever he called her and did whatever he wanted. She too made no secret of anything. She remembered how Harry had once told her 'You don't say no to a person like him' and found it to be true.

The Nawab was delighted with Olivia's pregnancy. He often stroked her slender hips, her small flat unmarked abdomen and asked her 'Really you will do this for me?' It seemed to strike him with wonder. 'You are not afraid? Oh how brave you are!' His surprise made her laugh.

He never for a moment doubted that the child was his. The question simply did not arise for him so that Olivia – for whom it arose constantly – did not even dare to mention it. He became possessive about her, and every evening, when it was time for the car to take her back, he did his best to delay her, even begging her to stay with him longer. She hated it when he did that, and then it would be she who would plead with him to let her go. And he said 'All right, go' but was so downcast that every time it became more difficult for her. Yet she had no choice. She dreaded the hour when it would be time for her to leave and he would say 'No. Stay.'

Once he said 'No. Stay with me. Stay always.' Then he said 'It has to be, very soon now. You have to be here.' He was very positive.

She knew that if she asked 'And Douglas?' he would answer her with a dismissive gesture: because as far as he was concerned Douglas had already been dismissed.

One Sunday an English chaplain came from Ambala and held a service in the little church. Afterwards Olivia and Douglas lingered behind in the churchyard; they had not visited it since that day they had quarrelled

2 **acknowledge sb./sth.**: recognise sb./sth. 19 **delay sb.**: jdn. aufhalten
21 **downcast**: sad and discouraged 28 **dismissive**: wegwerfend, abweisend
30 **chaplain**: minister, priest

there. It was very different now. Although the sun was still hot, the trees were no longer dusty but damp and dripping green. Showers of rain had also washed the dust off the graves so that the lettering stood out clearer now and tufts of green sprouted from the cracks in the stone.

Douglas, striding between the graves, read out the by now familiar inscriptions. He was so engrossed that he went too quickly for Olivia and she had to call out to him. He looked back and saw her come towards him in her pale mauve dress with flounced skirt and matching parasol. He hurried towards her and embraced her right there among the graves. They walked on together arm in arm. He told her about all these young men buried here, and then about other young men, his own ancestors, lying in graveyards in other parts of India. 'Great chaps,' he called them. There was Edward Rivers who had been one of Henry Lawrence's band of young administrators in the Punjab; John Rivers, a famous pig-sticker, killed in a fall from his horse at Meerut; and a namesake, an earlier Douglas Rivers who had died in the Mutiny. He had been present at the storming of the Kashmere Gate in which the Hero of Delhi, John Nicholson, also fell. Douglas' ancestor died of his wounds just a day after Nicholson and was buried very near him in the Nicholson cemetery at Delhi. The way Douglas said that made Olivia tease him: 'You sound as if you envy him.'

'Well,' said Douglas, feeling a bit sheepish, 'it's not a bad way to go ... Better than to drink yourself to death,' he said, attempting a lighter tone. 'Some of them did that too. It can get very tedious if you're stuck out too long in a district all on your own.'

'With only a few million Indians,' Olivia could not refrain from saying – but just then they reached the Saunders' angel and Douglas was very concerned to take her attention off that. He pressed her head against his shoulder and did not release her until they had passed that spot and

2 **damp**: slightly wet 3 **lettering** (n): Schrift 4 **sprout**: sprießen
6 **be engrossed**: in Gedanken versunken sein 8 **mauve**: a type of violet **flounced skirt**: mit Spitze besetzter Rock 9 **parasol**: umbrella that protects against sunlight
12 **chap** (infml): man 15 **pig-sticker**: person who hunts boars (= Wildschwein)
16 **namesake**: someone with the same name 21 **tease sb.**: jdn. necken
24 **tedious** ['ti:diəs]: tiring, boring 26 **refrain from doing sth.**: sich davon abhalten etwas zu tun

reached Lt. Edwards. Here he made her stop because that grave was shaded by a tree. They stood under its shelter.

'*Kind and indulgent Father*,' Douglas read. He turned to kiss Olivia and murmured to her 'Would you prefer a soldier or a civilian?'

'How do you know it will be a he?'

'Oh I'm pretty sure … And he'll do something decent too, you'll see.' He kissed her again and ran his hands along her slender hips and her flat abdomen. 'You're not afraid?' he whispered. 'You'll really do this for me? How brave you are.'

He thought she was upset because of the proximity of the Saunders' grave. Or perhaps the whole place had a bad effect on her – graveyards were morbid, of course, and especially for someone in her condition. As so often in his dealings with her – so much finer, frailer, he felt, than he or anyone he knew of – he accused himself of being a clumsy oaf and could not get her out of the place fast enough.

* * * *

20 August. Douglas did have a son – not by Olivia but by his second wife, Tessie. This son (my father) was born in India and lived there till he was 12 when he was sent to school in England. He never returned to India: by the time he was old enough to do so, there was nothing for him to return to. Instead he went into the antique business. At the time of Indian Independence Douglas, who had just reached retirement age, went home along with everyone else. He and Tessie had talked it over seriously whether they should go or stay on to spend their years of retirement in India. Several of their acquaintances had decided to stay on – those who, like themselves, had spent the best part of their lives here and loved the place above every other. Tessie's sister Beth and her husband had bought a charming cottage in Kasauli to settle down there, they thought, for the remainder of their lives. However, after some years they found it was no longer as pleasant for them as it had been. The Indianisation of India was of course highly desirable, said the Crawfords – ever fair-minded and seeing all sides of a question: but it was desirable

10 **proximity**: nearness 13 **frail**: fragile, tender 14 **clumsy oaf**: Tollpatsch, Trampel 27 **Kasauli**: hill town in north India, near Simla

for Indians rather than for the Crawfords themselves. They too came home and bought a house in Surrey near enough to Douglas and Tessie for frequent visits. After they were both left widows, Grandmother Tessie moved in with Great-Aunt Beth, bringing her own favourite things so that there was some duplication of brass table tops and ivory elephant tusks. For as long as possible they remained in touch with friends in India – the Minnies, for instance, lived in Ooty – but slowly, one by one, everyone died or grew too old to keep up contacts. I would have liked to look some of them up now that I have at last got here, but I don't think there is anyone left.

I tried to tell Chid some of all this, thinking it might interest him, but it doesn't. His own family never had any connection with India, and as far as he knows he is the first member of it ever to come out here. He is now very anxious to leave. But his health doesn't seem to be getting any better, and yesterday I persuaded him to come to the hospital with me. Dr. Gopal, the Medical Superintendent, examined him and said at once he would like to admit him. Chid agreed – I don't know what he had in mind, perhaps he saw himself resting amid cool sheets in a whitewashed room, tended by nuns. The reality turned out different. The doctor called one of his subordinates and questioned him about empty beds. There weren't any but one was expected to be free within an hour as an old man was dying. He did die within that time and I helped Chid to the ward and into the bed.

27 August. I visit Chid every day, both to keep him company and to bring him food. It is impossible for him to eat the hospital food which is doled out by an orderly passing along the ward with a bucket. The patients sit in rows holding out bowls into which are thrown lumps of cold rice and lentils and sometimes some vegetables all mixed up together. Only people who are completely destitute will accept this food, and it is indeed served up with the contempt reserved for those who have nothing and no one.

2 **Surrey**: county in south England 5 **table top**: Tischplatte **ivory**: Elfenbein 6 **tusk**: tooth of an elephant 7 **Ooty**: hill station in south India 14 **anxious to do sth.**: wanting very much to do sth. 18 **amid**: in the middle of 20 **subordinate**: Untergebene/r 26 **dole out sth.**: etwas austeilen, verteilen 28 **lentils**: Linsen

There is one such poor man lying with a broken leg and ribs next to Chid. He has told me that he came to Satipur from his village some years ago and has been making a living by selling fruit from a basket. He had always been hoping to earn enough to send for his family, but this has not happened so far and he reckons himself lucky to make enough to feed himself from day to day. He usually sleeps, together with other destitutes, under one of the old gateways leading out of Satipur. That is where he will go back to when his leg and ribs are mended. It is unfortunately taking a long time. What bothers him most is his inability to get up and around – his leg has been strapped up in a contraption – so that he is dependent for his natural functions on the hospital sweepers. At times they come and push a bedpan under him, but since he is not in a position to pay them even the humble sum they exact, they are not too punctual about providing this amenity nor about removing it from under him. Once I came and found him in great distress because he had been left there for several hours. I removed it from under him and went to empty it in a bathroom. The state of these latrines has to be seen to be believed, and when I came out I did feel a bit sick. I tried to hide this so as not to hurt anyone's feelings, but it seems I had already done enough. Everyone looked at me as if I had committed some terrible act of pollution, and the fruit man himself also shrank from me so that when as usual I offered him some of the food I had brought he refused it.

Chid takes no notice of his surroundings at all. In fact, he does his best to shut them out completely. Whenever I visit him, he is lying with his eyes tightly closed and sometimes tears trickle out of them. I have already written to his family to ask for a ticket home for him, and now we are both waiting for it to arrive and for his health to improve sufficiently for him to travel. Meanwhile he wants to know and see nothing; just to lie there and wait.

I still don't know what happened to change him this way. All he will ever say – the only explanation he gives for his changed feelings towards India – is how he can't stand the smell. I don't even know what's wrong

8 **mend sth.**: heal sth. 10 **contraption**: apparatus 11 **hospital sweeper**: Putzfrau/-mann im Krankenhaus 12 **bedpan**: Bettschüssel 13 **exact sth.** (fml): demand sth. 14 **amenity** [ə'mi:nəti]: comfort 21 **shrink from sb**: vor jdm. zurückschrecken

with him physically, what disease it is he has got. I asked Dr. Gopal and he couldn't tell me very clearly either. There is something wrong with Chid's liver and something else with his kidneys and altogether his insides are in a terrible state. It is due, said Dr. Gopal, to bad wrong food and to bad wrong living.

'You see,' he tried to explain – busy as he is, he always welcomes English conversation – 'this climate does not suit you people too well. And let alone you people, it does not suit even us.' He explained to me that not only Westerners but even most Indians suffer from amoebic dysentery. They hardly know it, for they also suffer from many other diseases. He became eloquent as he enumerated all the diseases of India. It was indeed a terrible roll call, and by the time he came to the end of it (if there is an end), he said 'I think perhaps God never meant that human beings should live in such a place.'

Here I contradicted him, and we had a discussion on this theme in English. He has already told me that, while at medical college, he was a member of the Debating Society and distinguished himself at several inter-University debates. He is indeed skilled at spicing truth with humour, and this is how he concluded our discussion:

'Let us admit for the sake of our argument that we Indians are fit to live here – where else are we fit for?' he asked, leaving a pause for me to laugh in. 'But no one else,' he said. 'None of you. You know in the bad old days you had your Clubs and they were reserved for British only? Well now it is like this that we have our germs and we have reserved these for ourselves only. For Indians only! Keep out!' He threw himself back in his chair to laugh and was still laughing as he turned to jab a needle into an emaciated arm that was held out to him.

Of course to some extent I have to admit he is right: certainly as far as Chid is concerned. Obviously Chid's body is not made to live the life of an Indian holy man. And it is not only physically that Chid is out of action, but in other ways – spiritually – too. Do the doctor's strictures apply to the European soul as well as our bodies? I don't want to admit it; I don't want it to be so. There have been people in the past who

3 **kidney**: Niere 12 **roll call**: Aufzählung, Auflistung 18 **spice sth.**: etwas würzen 24 **germs** (pl): Bazillen 26–27 **jab sth. into sth.**: insert sth. (esp. a needle) into sth. 27 **emaciated** (adj): very thin 31 **strictures** (pl): scharfe Kritik

stayed on here of their own free will. After the Mutiny an anonymous Englishman continued to live all by himself outside the gates of Lucknow, doing religious penance. Another anonymous Englishman was seen for years moving around the bazaars of Multan dressed up as an Afghan horse dealer (no one ever discovered who he was or where he came from, and eventually he was found murdered). And what about the woman missionary I had met on my first night in Bombay? She said she had been in India for thirty years and was prepared to die here if called upon to do so. Yes, and what about Olivia? It seems ludicrous to bracket her with religious seekers, adventurers, and Christian missionaries: yet, like them, she stayed.

I still don't think there was anything very special about Olivia; I mean, that she started off with any very special qualities. When she first came here, she may really have been what she seemed; a pretty young woman, rather vain, pleasure-seeking, a little petulant. Yet to have done what she did – and then to have stuck to it all her life long – she couldn't have remained the same person she had been. But there is no record of what she became later, neither in our family nor anywhere else as far as I know. More and more I want to find out; but I suppose the only way I can is to do the same as she did – that is, stay on.

1923

The landscape which, a few weeks earlier, had been blotted out by dust was now hazy with moisture. The view from Harry's window was shrouded by clouds so that everything was seen as through tears that did not fall. The resulting air of sadness matched Harry's mood. He told Olivia 'I had a long talk with him yesterday. I told him I wanted to go home, that I *had* to ... And he agreed. He understood completely. He said he'd make all the arrangements, I was to travel first class, everything must be – tiptop.'

Olivia smiled: 'I can hear him say that.'

3 **penance**: Buße 9 **ludicrous**: ridiculous 9–10 **bracket sb.with sb.**: jdn. mit jdm. gleichsetzen 15 **petulant**: launisch 17 **record**: written information 22 **blotted out**: ausradiert 23 **hazy** ['heɪzi]: dunstig, diesig

'Yes.' Harry too smiled through his sadness. 'And he made me a declaration.'

'I think I can hear that too.'

'Yes you can. Of course it's always the same – but Olivia it's *always true*! Don't you feel that? That when he holds his heart the way he does it's because he really means it? … He talked about you too. Oh don't think I feel bad about anything. Good Lord, what sort of a person would I be then, what sort of a friend? I wouldn't be – worthy of him, would I.'

Olivia said 'Where is he?'

'In Indore. Yesterday he heard from Simla – they are threatening an enquiry and he sat up all night composing telegrams and this morning he drove off to Indore to consult his lawyers.'

'Is it true, Harry? Is he involved with them?'

'Goodness knows. As far as I'm concerned, he's always right and they're wrong. I hate them. They're the sort of people who've made life hell for me ever since I can remember. At school and everywhere. Well as long as they stick to bullying me – but when I see them doing it to *him* – and *here* – no that's unbearable. And he won't bear it. They'll find out. You should have heard him last night. Wait till my son is born, he said; then they'll laugh from the other side of their mouths.'

'He said that?'

She turned from the window and stared at him so that he knew at once that he had said too much.

'What else did he say?' she asked. 'No now you have to tell me. I have to hear.'

'You know how often he says things he doesn't mean. When he's excited like that.' But the way she went on staring at him, he had to continue: 'He said when this baby was born, Douglas and all were going to have the shock of their lives.'

'Did he mean – the colour?' Then she said 'How is he so sure?' She looked at Harry: 'You are too, aren't you … You think he's a – irresistible force of nature –'

'Don't you?'

12 **enquiry**: investigation

She turned back to the window. She stuck out her hand to see if the rain had started. It had, but so softly that it was both invisible and inaudible, and everything – the garden pavilions, the pearl-grey walls, the mosque – seemed to be dissolving of its own accord like sugar in water.

'I've been thinking about having an abortion,' she said.

'Are you quite crazy.'

'Douglas is terribly happy too. And making all sorts of plans. There's a christening robe in their family that was worked by some nuns in Goa. His sister has it at the moment – her littlest one was christened in it a couple of years ago, at Quetta where they're stationed. But now Douglas is going to send for it. He says it's awfully pretty. Cascades of white lace – very becoming to the Rivers' babies who are very very fair. Douglas says they all have white-blond hair till they're about twelve.'

'Babies don't have hair.'

'Indian babies do, I've seen them. They're born with lots of black hair … You have to help me, Harry. You have to find out where I can go.' When he stood dumb, she said: 'Ask your friend the Begum. It'll be easy enough for her.' She laughed: 'Easier than poisoned garments, any day,' she said.

* * * *

31 August. Today, as I came down from my room, a woman standing outside the slipper shop greeted me like an old acquaintance. I didn't remember meeting her but thought she might be a friend of Inder Lal's mother; perhaps one of the group of women who had accompanied us on the Husband's Wedding Day. When I walked away through the bazaar, she followed me. It now struck me that perhaps she had been waiting for me outside the shop; but when I stood still and looked back at her, she made no attempt to catch up with me. She just nodded and smiled. This happened several times. She even made signs at me to walk on; all she seemed to want was to walk behind me. I had intended to go

3 **inaudible**: not hearable 4 **dissolve**: disappear **of your own accord**: von selbst 9 **christening robe**: Taufkleid 13 **be becoming to sb.**: suit sb. 18 **dumb** (old-fashioned): unable to speak

all the way to the hospital, but I felt strange being followed, so when I got to the royal tombs I turned aside and made my way to Maji's hut. This time when I looked back, the woman was not following me but was walking straight on as if she had no further business with me.

Maji was in the state of *samadhi*. To be in that state means to have reached a higher level of consciousness and to be submerged in its bliss. At such times Maji is entirely unaware of anything going on around her. She sits on the floor in the lotus pose; her eyes are open but the pupils turned up, her lips slightly parted with the tip of the tongue showing between them. Her breathing is regular and peaceful as in dreamless sleep.

When she woke up – if that's the right expression which it isn't – she smiled at me in welcome as if nothing at all had occurred. But, as always at such times, she was like a person who has just stepped out of a revivifying bath, or some other medium of renewal. Her cheeks glowed and her eyes shone. She passed her hands upwards over her face as if she felt it flushed and fiery. She has told me that, whereas it used to be very difficult for her to make the transition from *samadhi* back to ordinary life, now it is quite easy and effortless.

When I spoke to her about the woman who had so mysteriously followed me, she said 'You see, it has started.' Apparently it wasn't mysterious at all – the woman was a midwife marking me down as a potential client. She must have noticed me before and followed me today to check up on her suspicions. My condition would be perfectly obvious to her by the way I walked and held myself. In a day or two she would probably offer me her services. And now Maji offered me her own again: 'This would be a good time,' she said. '8 or 9 weeks – it would not be too difficult.'

'How would you do it?' I asked, almost in idle curiosity. She explained that there were several ways, and that at this early stage a simple massage, skilfully applied, might do it. 'Would you like me to try?' she asked.

I said yes – again I think just out of curiosity. Maji shut the door of her hut. It wasn't a real door but a plank of wood someone had given her. I lay down on the floor, and she loosened the string of my Punjabi

6 **submerged**: versunken 15 **revivify**: gain new energy 22 **mark sb. down as sth.**: think of sb. as sth.

trousers. 'Don't be afraid,' she said. I wasn't, not at all. I lay looking up at the roof which was a sheet of tin, and at the mud walls blackened from her cooking fire. Now, with the only aperture closed, it was quite dark inside and all sorts of smells were sealed in – of dampness, the cowdung used as fuel, and the lentils she had cooked; also of Maji herself. Her only change of clothes hung on the wall, unwashed.

She sat astride me. I couldn't see her clearly in the dark, but she seemed larger than life and made me think of some mythological figure: one of those potent Indian goddesses who hold life and death in one hand and play them like a yo-yo. Her hands passed slowly down my womb, seeking out and pressing certain parts within. She didn't hurt me – on the contrary, her hands seemed to have a kind of soothing quality. They were very, very hot; they are always so, I have felt them often (she is always touching one, as if wanting to transmit something). But today they seemed especially hot, and I thought this might be left over from her *samadhi*, that she was still carrying the waves of energy that had come to her from elsewhere. And again I had the feeling of her *transmitting* something to me – not taking away, but giving.

Nevertheless I suddenly cried out 'No please stop!' She did so at once. She got off me and took the plank of wood from the door. Light streamed in. I got up and went outside, into that brilliant light. The rain had made everything shining green and wet. Blue tiles glinted on the royal tombs and everywhere there were little hollows of water that caught the light and looked like precious stones scattered over the landscape. The sky shone in patches of monsoon blue through puffs of cloud, and in the distance more clouds, but of a very dark blue, were piled on each other like weightless mountains.

'Nothing will happen, will it?' I asked Maji anxiously. She had followed me out of the hut and was no longer the dark mythological figure she had been inside but her usual, somewhat bedraggled motherly self. She laughed when I asked that and patted my cheek in reassurance.

2 **tin**: Zinn 3 **aperture**: opening (e.g. a window) 5 **cowdung**: excrement of a cow **fuel**: Brennstoff 7 **astride**: rittlings (auf) 12 **soothing** (adj): wohltuend, entspannend 22 **glint**: glitzern 23 **hollow**: hole 25–26 **puffs of cloud**: Wolkenfetzen, Wölkchen 30 **bedraggled** (adj): ungepflegt 31 **pat sb./sth.**: touch sb./sth. gently several times

But I didn't know what she was reassuring me of. Above all I wanted nothing to happen – that her efforts should not prove successful. It was absolutely clear to me now that I wanted my pregnancy and the completely new feeling – of rapture – of which it was the cause.

1923

Satipur also had its slummy lanes, but Khatm had nothing else. The town huddled in the shadow of the Palace walls in a tight knot of dirty alleys with ramshackle houses leaning over them. There were open gutters flowing through the streets. They often overflowed, especially during the rains, and were probably the cause, or one of them, of the frequent epidemics that broke out in Khatm. If it rained rather more heavily, some of the older houses would collapse and bury the people inside them. This happened regularly every year.

It had happened the week before opposite the house to which Olivia was taken. The women attending on her were still talking about it. One of them described how she had stood on the balcony to watch a wedding procession passing below. When the bridegroom rode by, everyone surged forward to see him, and there was so much noise, she said, the band was playing so loudly, that at first she had not realised what was happening though it was happening before her eyes. She saw the house opposite, which she had known all her life, suddenly cave inwards and disintegrate, and next moment everything came crashing and flying through the air in a shower of people, bricks, tiles, furniture, cooking pots. It had been, she said, like a dream, a terrible dream.

What was happening to Olivia was also like a dream. Although no one could have been more matter-of-fact than the women attending her: two homely, middle-aged midwives doing the job they had been commissioned for. The maid servant who had brought her had also been quite matter-of-fact. She had dressed Olivia in a burqa and made her follow her on foot through the lanes of Khatm. No one took any notice

4 **rapture**: extreme joy 8 **ramshackle**: looking as if ready to collapse 17 **bridegroom**: Bräutigam 18 **surge forward**: vorwärtsdrängen 23 **brick**: Backstein **tile**: Ziegel 27 **homely**: warm and friendly 27–28 **be commissioned for sth.**: mit etwas beauftragt sein

of them – they were just two women in burqas, the usual walking tents. The street of the midwives was reached by descending some slippery steps (here Olivia, unused to her burqa, had to be particularly careful). The midwives' house was in a tumble-down condition – very likely it would go in the next monsoon; the stairs looked especially dangerous. They were so dark that her escort had to take Olivia's hand – for a moment Olivia shrank from this physical contact but only for a moment, knowing that soon she would be touched in a far more intimate manner and in more intimate places.

The midwives made her lie on a mat on the floor. Since the house opposite was no longer there, she had a clear view through the window of a patch of sky. She tried to concentrate on that and not on what they were doing to her. But this was in any case not unpleasant. They were massaging her abdomen in an enormously skilful way, seeking out and pressing certain veins within. One of the women sat astride her while the other squatted on the floor. Their hands worked over her incessantly while they carried on their conversation. The atmosphere was professional and relaxed. But when sounds were heard on the stairs, the two midwives looked at each other in consternation. One of them went to the door, and the other quickly hid Olivia under a sheet. As if I'm dead, Olivia thought. She wondered who had come. Also she wondered what would happen – what would they do – if she did die there in the room as a result of the abortion. They would have to dispose of her body quickly and secretly. Olivia guessed that such a disposal could be managed without too much difficulty. The Begum would arrange about it just as easily as she had arranged for the abortion. Probably she had already thought about it and laid suitable plans.

It was the Begum herself who had come, with only one attendant. Both of them were shrouded in black burqas but Olivia knew which was the Begum from the deferential way in which the midwives treated her. She appeared keenly interested in the operation (such personal attention, Olivia thought; I ought to be flattered). The Begum watched from behind her burqa as the two midwives continued their massage.

4 **tumble-down**: baufällig 15 **vein**: Vene 19 **consternation**: shock, worry
23 **dispose of sth.**: get rid of sth. 29 **shrouded**: covered with a single cloth
30 **deferential**: respektvoll

Then one of them got up and went to prepare something in a corner of the room. Olivia tried to see what it was, and the Begum was also curious and followed to that corner. Olivia lifted her head slightly but the other midwife pressed it down again so she only swivelled her eyes in that direction. She saw the midwife showing the Begum a twig on to which she was rubbing some paste. The Begum was so interested that she put up the front of her burqa in order to see better. Now Olivia was curious to see both the twig and the Begum's face. She had forgotten what she looked like – that visit with Mrs. Crawford seemed long ago – and wanted to check up whether she had any resemblance to the Nawab.

The midwife with the twig came towards her, holding it. Olivia understood that it was to be introduced into herself. The two women opened Olivia's legs and one of them held on to her ankles while the other pointed the twig. The Begum also bent over her to watch. Although the midwife worked swiftly and skilfully, the twig hurt Olivia as it entered into her. She was unable to stifle a cry. Then the Begum bent over her to look into her face and Olivia stared back at her. She *did* look like the Nawab, very much. She seemed as interested to study Olivia's face as Olivia was to study hers. For a moment they gazed into each other's eyes and then Olivia had to shut hers, as the pain down below was repeated.

* * * *

Beth Crawford did not allow herself to speak about Olivia until many years – a lifetime – had passed. I don't know whether she thought about her at all during those years. Probably not: Great-Aunt Beth knew where lines had to be drawn, not only in speech and behaviour but also in one's thought. In the same way she had never let her mind dwell on the Begum and her ladies once the half-hour of obligatory social intercourse

4 **swivel sth.**: turn sth. 5 **twig**: Zweig 17 **stifle a cry** ['staɪfəl]: einen Schrei unterdrücken 26 **draw lines**: Grenzen ziehen 27 **dwell on sth.**: think about sth. for a long time 28 **social intercourse**: everything you do in a group, e.g. conversation, having tea or coffee, etc.

with them was over. She had had no desire to speculate about what went on in those purdah quarters once she had left them behind and the European chairs were put away and the ladies alone again and at ease on their divans. Beth felt that there were oriental privacies – mysteries – that should not be disturbed, whether they lay within the Palace, the bazaar of Satipur, or the alleys of Khatm. All those dark regions were outside her sphere of action or imagination – as was Olivia once she had crossed over into them.

The only person not to be reticent about Olivia was Dr. Saunders. It was he who had found her out. The midwives at Khatm had done their work well, and Olivia began to miscarry that same night. She woke up Douglas who took her to the hospital, and early next morning Dr. Saunders curetted her. But he knew about Indian 'miscarriages' and the means employed to bring them about. The most common of these was the insertion of a twig smeared with the juice of a certain plant known only to Indian midwives. In his time Dr. Saunders had extracted many such twigs from women brought to him with so-called miscarriages. Afterwards he confronted the guilty women and threw them out of the hospital. Sometimes he slapped them – he had strong ideas about morality and how to uphold it. But even he admitted that certain allowances might be made for these native women born in ignorance and dirt. There was no such extenuating circumstance for Olivia. 'Now my young madam,' he said as he confronted her. The matron, a Scottish woman born in India – between them, she and Dr. Saunders kept the hospital clean and strict – stood grimfaced behind him. Both were outraged, but Dr. Saunders was somewhat triumphant as well, having been proved right. He had always known that there was something rotten about Olivia: something weak and rotten which of course the Nawab (rotten himself) had found out and used to his advantage.

No one ever doubted that the Nawab had used Olivia as a means of revenge. Even the most liberal and sympathetic Anglo-Indian, such as

4 **privacy**: Privatbereich 9 **reticent**: quiet and discrete 11 **miscarry**: eine Fehlgeburt haben 13 **curet sb.**: (here) remove the dead fetus 16 **extract sth.**: etwas herausziehen 20 **allowance**: Zugeständnis 22 **extenuating circumstance**: mildernder Umstand 23 **matron** ['meɪtrən]: Oberschwester 25 **outraged** (adj): shocked and angry

Major Minnies, was convinced of it. Like the Crawfords, and presumably Douglas himself (who allowed no one to guess his feelings), Major Minnies banished Olivia from his thoughts. She had gone in too far. Yet for many years he reflected not so much on her particular case as on its implications. It all fitted in with his theories. Later, during his retirement in Ooty, he had a lot more time to think about the whole question, and he even published – at his own expense, it was not a subject of much general interest – a monograph on the influence of India on the European consciousness and character. He sent it around to his friends, and that was how Great-Aunt Beth had a copy which I read.

Although the Major was so sympathetic to India, his piece sounds like a warning. He said that one has to be very determined to withstand – to stand up to – India. And the most vulnerable, he said, are always those who love her best. There are many ways of loving India, many things to love her for – the scenery, the history, the poetry, the music, and indeed the physical beauty of the men and women – but all, said the Major, are dangerous for the European who allows himself to love too much. India always, he said, finds out the weak spot and presses on it. Both Dr. Saunders and Major Minnies spoke of the weak spot. But whereas for Dr. Saunders it is something, or someone, rotten, for the Major this weak spot is to be found in the most sensitive, often the finest people – and, moreover, in their finest feelings. It is there that India seeks them out and pulls them over into what the Major called the other dimension. He also referred to it as another element, one in which the European is not accustomed to live so that by immersion in it he becomes debilitated, or even (like Olivia) destroyed. Yes, concluded the Major, it is all very well to love and admire India – intellectually, aesthetically, he did not mention sexually but he must have been aware of that factor too – but always with a virile, measured, *European* feeling. One should never, he warned, allow oneself to become softened (like Indians) by an excess of feeling; because the moment that happens – the moment

1 **presumably**: probably 3 **banish sb./sth.**: jdn./etwas verbannen, vertreiben 5 **implication**: consequence 8 **monograph**: short academic book 12 **withstand sth.**: resist sth. 13 **vulnerable**: verwundbar 25 **be accustomed to sth.**: be used to sth. **immersion**: Eintauchen, Untertauchen 26 **debilitated** (adj): weakened 29 **virile**: manly

one exceeds one's measure – one is in danger of being dragged over to the other side. That seems to be the last word Major Minnies had to say on the subject and his final conclusion. He who loved India so much, knew her so well, chose to spend the end of his days here! But she always remained for him an opponent, even sometimes an enemy, to be guarded and if necessary fought against from without and, especially, from within: from within one's own being.

Olivia never returned to Douglas but, escaping from the hospital, she went straight to the Palace. The last clear picture I have of her is not from her letters but from what Harry has told us. He was in the Palace when she arrived there from the hospital. She was so pale, he said, that she seemed drained of blood. (Of course she had suffered great blood loss from her abortion.) It isn't so very far from Satipur to Khatm – about 15 miles – and it was a journey that she had been doing daily by one of the Nawab's cars. But that time when she ran away from the hospital there was no car. Harry never knew how she came but presumed it was by what he called some native mode of transport. She was also in native dress – a servant's coarse sari – so that she reminded him of a print he had seen called *Mrs. Secombe in Flight from the Mutineers*. Mrs. Secombe was also in native dress and in a state of great agitation, with her hair awry and smears of dirt on her face: naturally, since she was flying for her life from the mutineers at Sikrora to the safety of the British Residency at Lucknow. Olivia was also in flight – but, as Harry pointed out, in the opposite direction.

Harry left India shortly afterwards. He never had been able to decide what were the Nawab's motives in taking on Olivia. In any case, the question – like the Nawab himself – dropped out of Harry's view for many years. He was glad. When he looked back on his time spent in the Palace, it was always with dislike, even sometimes with abhorrence. Yet he had been very, very happy there. Back in England he felt that it had been a happiness too strong for him. Now he wanted only to lead his quiet life with his mother in their flat in Kensington. Later, after his

1 **exceed your measure**: (here) go beyond what is good for you 11 **pale**: bleich 12 **be drained of sth.**: be emptied of sth. 18 **coarse**: rough 20 **agitation**: Aufregung 21 **awry** [əˈraɪ]: in a mess 29 **abhorrence**: Abscheu

mother died, his friend Ferdie moved in with him, giving up his job in a laundry in order to look after Harry. Ferdie also met the Nawab, but that was many years later by which time – Harry thought – the Nawab was quite changed. His circumstances were changed too, and when he came to London now, he no longer lived at Claridges but was quite hard up. Perhaps that was why he never brought Olivia, because he couldn't afford it; or perhaps she just didn't want to come. She never came to England again but stayed in the house in the mountains he had bought for her.

When I told Maji that I was leaving Satipur, she asked 'Like Chid?' Chid's departure back to England had amused her as everything else about him had always amused her. 'Poor boy,' she said. 'He had to run away.' Her broad shoulders shook with laughter.

I assured her that I was not running away but on the contrary was going further, up into the mountains. She was pleased with that. I then plucked up courage and asked her, as I had wanted to for some time, what she had been doing to me that day when she said she was giving me an abortion. To my relief nothing had happened – but I felt that, if she had wanted something to happen, her efforts would not have been unsuccessful. What *had* she done? I asked her. Of course she wouldn't tell me, but from her sly laugh I gathered that she was not innocent. I thought of the way she had sat astride me, a supernatural figure with supernatural powers which it now seemed to me she had used not to terminate my pregnancy but to make sure of it: make sure I saw it through.

The rainy season is not the best time of year to go up into the mountains. There are always landslides and the roads become impassable for days on end. The mountains are invisible. One knows they are there – the ranges of the Himalayas stretching God knows into what distances and to what heights – one even feels, or imagines, their presence, but

5–6 **be hard up** (infml): have no money 16 **pluck up courage**: Mut fassen
21 **sly**: verschlagen **gather**: folgern 27 **landslide**: Erdrutsch
impassable: that cannot be passed or driven through

they can't be seen. They are completely blotted out and in their place are clouds, vapours, mists.

Just above the small town of X, there is a handful of houses scattered along the steepest side of the mountain. Even at the best of times they are difficult to get to except by the sturdiest climbers; and now during the rains they are almost inaccessible. I have been told that, up till a few years ago, there were several other Europeans besides Olivia living in these houses. The Norwegian widow of an Indian historian devoting herself to sorting out her husband's papers; a German turned Buddhist; and two ex-missionaries who had tried to start a Christian 'ashram'. Now they are all dead and are buried in the old British cemetery on a plateau a few hundred feet down (there are British cemeteries everywhere! they have turned out to be the most lasting monument). Only the German Buddhist was cremated on the Hindu cremation ground, and Olivia. The ex-missionaries tried to raise some objection to Olivia's cremation – they said she belonged in the cemetery, never having been converted to any Indian religion. But she had specifically requested cremation, so it was done. I presume that her ashes were scattered over these mountains since there was no one to take charge of them, the Nawab having died before her.

Her house is still there. I had to wait several days for the rain to clear sufficiently before I could climb up. It stands quite by itself on a mountain ledge; I suppose it has a superb view, though at this time of year there is nothing to view except, as I said, clouds. There is some dispute about possession of the house which Karim and Kitty are trying to get settled along with other disputed properties of the Nawab's. They hope to do so before the Army requisitions the house. It has developed dangerous cracks, and inside everything is covered in mildew.

But it retains what I imagine to have been Olivia's ambience. There is a piano of course – not the upright she had in Satipur but a grand piano

2 **vapour** ['veɪpə]: Dampf, Dunst 5 **sturdy**: strong and healthy 6 **inaccessible**: that cannot be reached 10 **ashram**: (usu. in Hinduism) centre for spiritual learning and religious practice 23 **ledge**: Felsvorsprung 25 **dispute**: argument 27 **requisition sth.**: etwas beschlagnahmen 28 **mildew**: Moder 29 **retain sth.**: keep sth. alive

the Nawab had sent up from Khatm (together with the tuner from Bombay). The curtains and cushions, now tattered, are yellow, the lampshades tasselled; there is a gramophone. A chair and embroidery frame stand in a window embrasure: I don't know whether this is just a decorative tableau or whether she actually used to sit here, glancing up from her embroidery to look out over the mountains (now invisible). There is a row of stables outside but all they ever stabled was the sedan chair – it is still there, though dusty and broken – in which the Nawab was carried up and down the mountain. He had got too fat and lazy to climb.

Harry said that he had a shock when he saw him again in London. Fifteen years had passed, the Nawab was fifty years old and so fat that there was something womanly about him. And the way he embraced Harry was womanly too: he held him against his plump chest with both arms and kept him there for a long time. And then all the old feelings came back to Harry. But afterwards he found that his feelings towards the Nawab *had* changed – probably because the Nawab himself had changed so much. He seemed softer and milder, and with many troubles of a domestic nature.

The court of enquiry set up in 1923 had gone against him, and as a result a prime minister had been appointed to take charge of the affairs of Khatm. Although still in name the ruler of the state, the Nawab did not under these circumstances care to spend much time there. The Begum too was not often in residence but had taken a house in Bombay for herself and her ladies. The Nawab often stayed with them there, when he was not with Olivia in X. Sometimes he also stayed with his wife, Sandy, things having been more or less compounded with the Cabobpur family. But Sandy's health was not good, and at present she was in a place in Switzerland undergoing treatment for her mental troubles.

2 **tattered** (adj): worn out 3 **tasselled** (adj): mit Quasten versehen **embroidery**: Stickerei 4 **embrasure** (n): Scharte (Einschnitt) an einem Fenster 7–8 **sedan chair**: Sänfte 21 **take charge of sth.**: für etwas die Veantwortung übernehmen 27 **be compounded**: be settled

The Nawab's own troubles were mainly financial. Not only did he have to keep up the Palace and three separate establishments – for his mother, wife, and Olivia – but he still had many dependants in Khatm. He had to provide for all those young men – now young no longer – who had been his companions in the Palace, for they were either his blood relatives or descendants of family retainers some of whom went right back to the time of Amanullah Khan. The Nawab felt deeply ashamed of no longer being able to keep them in the manner to which they were accustomed. For years he had been haggling with the British authorities for an increase in the income they had stipulated for him out of the state revenues: but they were completely un-understanding, they had no conception at all of the obligations a ruler like himself had to discharge. That was why he had now come to London, in order to appeal directly to a higher authority. He made, or tried to make, many appointments and was for ever pulling scraps of paper out of his pocket with names and telephone numbers scribbled on them, though often he could not remember whose they were.

He spent most of his time with Harry and Ferdie. It was not easy for them. They lived in a very orderly way but he was not an orderly person. He also seemed physically too large for the flat, and in fact broke two of the dining room chairs just by sitting on them. And they had difficulty feeding him for he could not be satisfied on the meals Ferdie cooked for Harry's delicate digestion (which had never recovered from India). The Nawab had developed a sweet tooth and, unable to obtain Indian sweetmeats in London, had got into the habit of eating a great number of cream pastries. His afternoons were usually spent in a popular restaurant – a palatial hall with marble pillars not unlike the Palace at Khatm. Three times in the course of the afternoon a lady in a long tea gown played selections on a multicoloured organ; and listening to her with pleasure, the Nawab would turn to Harry: 'How nicely she plays - just like Olivia.' He had always been quite unmusical.

3 **dependant**: person who is financially dependent on sb. 9 **haggle with sb.**: mit jdm. feilschen 10 **stipulate sth. for sb.**: von jdm. etwas verlangen 12–13 **discharge obligations**: Verpflichtungen nachkommen 23 **delicate digestion**: empfindliche Verdauung 28–29 **tea gown**: afternoon dress 29 **selections**: pieces of music **organ**: Orgel

Like his father, he had in recent years become very fond of reciting Persian and Urdu couplets, especially those that dealt, as most of them did, with the transience of worldly glory. He would point to himself as a living illustration of this theme. Besides the question of increased allowance, his most urgent problem at the time was that of the state jewels which were missing. The government of Khatm was accusing the Begum of having purloined them: to which she answered with spirit that she had taken nothing that was not her own. This case was indeed destined to linger on for many years and, after Independence, became the problem of the Government of India who tried to bring a case against the Begum. However, by that time both she and the jewels were safely in New York.

The Nawab became excited when he spoke of the harassment offered to his mother. He suffered from high blood pressure, and when he got too worked up, Harry would try and calm him down. 'You'll have a fit of apoplexy and die', Harry warned him. (In fact this did happen – but not for another fifteen years and then it was in New York, in the Park Avenue apartment of the ancient Begum and in her arms.) When Harry said that, the Nawab always laughed: he truly did laugh at the thought of dying. He liked to tell a story of something that had happened in Khatm about a year after Harry's departure. The gang of dacoits with whom the Nawab had been suspected of associating had been rounded up by the (reformed) police force. Some of them had been killed in direct encounters, others had been captured and brought to trial. These were all sentenced to death for various murders and dacoities committed over the years. The Nawab visited them in prison many times and found them cheerful and resigned right up till the end. In fact, he spent their last night with them, watched them eat their last meal, play their last game of cards, lay themselves down to sleep. They actually slept – it was he who remained awake. He accompanied them to the place of execution and joined them in their last prayers. He watched the noose being placed around their necks and stayed till the very last moment. At that

3 **transience**: the fact that nothing lasts forever 5 **allowance**: Zuteilung
7 **purloin sth.** (fml): steal sth. 9 **linger on**: carry on in a slow way 13 **harassment**: Belästigung, Schikanierung 15–16 **fit of apoplexy**: Schlaganfall
31 **noose**: Schlinge

last moment, one of them – Tikku Ram, a man of very high caste – suddenly turned to the hangman and began to ask 'Are you a –?' but could not finish because the hangman had slipped the hood over his face. The missing word was probably '*chamar*' – he was worried about the caste of the hangman who was performing this last intimate function for him. It was apparently his only worry at that moment of departure. The Nawab commended this attitude and said he hoped he would be able to emulate its spirit when his turn came.

There are no glimpses of Olivia in later years. The Nawab did not speak about her very much: she had become as private a topic to him as the Begum. He never said anything about the way she was and lived up there in X. Perhaps he never thought about it, just assuming she was all right with the comforts he took care to provide for her. She herself gave no clues either. She still corresponded with Marcia but, unlike her letters from Satipur, the letters from X were short and quite unrevealing. Also very rare – at first she wrote two or three times a year, but even that grew less. She never wrote after the Nawab's death, though she survived him by six years.

Marcia told Harry that she and Olivia were very much alike. Harry thought this may have been true when they were young – Marcia too was small and frail though dark where Olivia had been blonde – but by the time he got to know Marcia he had difficulty in reconciling her with his memories of Olivia. Marcia drank and smoked too much, and laughed shrilly. She was talkative, nervous, and had twice taken an overdose of sleeping tablets. She said that where she and Olivia were most alike was in their temperament which was passionate. She claimed she could understand Olivia completely. Of course, she said, their tastes differed – for instance, Marcia never could understand what Olivia had seen in Douglas, as far as she, Marcia, was concerned, he was just a *stick* and she was not in the least surprised that Olivia should have got bored to death with him and gone off with someone more interesting. Later,

3 **hood**: Kapuze 4 **chamar** (Hindi): member of a low caste consisting of people working with leather 7 **commend sb./sth.**: praise sb./sth. 8 **emulate sth.** (fml): copy sth. 9 **glimpse**: flüchtiger Blick 22 **reconcile sb./sth. with sb./sth.**: jdn./etwas mit jdm./etwas in Einklang bringen 26 **passionate**: leidenschaftlich

when she met the Nawab in London, Marcia said that he *was* more interesting than Douglas, though again, personally speaking, not her type. But the fact that her and Olivia's tastes differed did not detract from the similarity of their temperaments; nor of their characters – which were prepared to follow the dictates of those temperaments wherever they might lead them. When Harry asked the Nawab whether Marcia was like Olivia, the Nawab said 'Oh no no no no!' without a moment's hesitation. The idea seemed to strike him as simultaneously ludicrous and horrifying.

What was she like? How did she live? Looking around her house above X, it strikes me that perhaps she did not live so very differently from the way she had done in Satipur, and might have done in London. The rooms were arranged in her style, she still played the same pieces of piano music. That much I learned from the remains of her house – though not much else. I still cannot imagine what she thought about all those years, or how she became. Unfortunately it was raining heavily all the time I was there, so I couldn't see what she looked out on as she sat in the window at her embroidery frame. It might make a difference to know that.

I have taken a room in the town of X and live there in the same way I did in Satipur. The town is the same too – the houses are ramshackle, the alleys intricate and narrow; only here everything is on a slope, so that it looks as if the whole town might slide down the mountain any minute. Bits of it do slide down from time to time, especially now during the rains; and the mountains themselves crumble off in chunks which hurtle down and block the sodden roads. I'm impatient for it to stop raining because I want to move on, go higher up. I keep looking up all the time, but everything remains hidden. Unable to see, I imagine mountain peaks higher than any I've ever dreamed of; the snow on them is also whiter than all other snow – so white it is luminous and shines against a sky which is of a deeper blue than any yet known to me.

3 **detract from sth.**: etwas beeinträchtigen 22 **slope**: Abhang 25 **crumble off**: fall off in small pieces **chunk**: piece 26 **hurtle down**: fall very fast **sodden** (adj): extremely wet 30 **luminous**: full of light

That is what I expect to see. Perhaps it is also what Olivia saw: the view – or vision – that filled her eyes all those years and suffused her soul.

I rarely look down. Sometimes, when the rains stop, the mist in the valley swirls about and afterwards the air is so drenched with moisture that the birds seem to swim about in it and the trees wave like sea weed. I think it will be a long time before I go down again. First of course I'm going to have my baby. There is a sort of ashram further up, and I'm told they might take me in. I have seen some of the swamis from the ashram when they come down to the bazaar to do their shopping. They are very much respected in the town because of the good lives they lead. They are completely dedicated to studying the philosophy of those ancient writings that had their birth up in the highest heights of these mountains I cannot yet see. The swamis are cheerful men and they laugh and joke in booming voices with the people in the bazaar. I'm told that any sincere seeker can go up to the ashram, and they will allow one to stay for as long as one wants. Only most people come down again quite soon because of the cold and the austere living conditions.

Next time I meet a swami I shall speak to him and ask for permission to come up. I don't know yet how long I shall stay. In any case, it will have to be some time because of my condition which will make it more and more difficult to get down again, even if I should want to.

2 **suffuse sth.**: etwas erfüllen, durchfluten 4 **drenched**: completely wet **moisture**: Feuchtigkeit 5 **sea weed**: Seetang 14 **booming** (adj): very loud 17 **austere**: simple

Additional Texts

1
A Day in the Life of a District Officer

We got up at five, drank a cup of tea while the horse was being brought, and I went for my ride. Governing men is grand work, the noblest of all occupations, though perhaps the most difficult. But as I acquired, gradually, more experience and greater familiarity with those small but essential matters of routine which hang about work, I began to feel my strength and enjoy my duties more.

Returning about 6.30, my wife and I had our regular early morning tea on the verandah; our little girls, who had been for a ride on their ponies, played around us. Then I went round our beautiful garden and gave orders. About seven, the post came in and we looked at our letters, discussed any matters requiring arrangements and read the paper, *The Englishmen*, the leading journal in Bengal in those days.

At ten, bath and breakfast, and off to court, a drive of three miles [...]. Our instructions were to decide all cases by the light of common sense and our own sense of what was just and right [...]. The public crowded into my large courtroom, and presented many petitions, each of which was read to me by a clerk and orders passed thereon.

Now followed interviews with the head clerks of each department. Each man brought those papers on which orders were required, took his orders and departed. I wrote replies to letters [...], but was usually interrupted by assistant collectors and other officials coming in to speak to me about this or that. Generally, however, by two o'clock the correspondence was finished. Whether it was or not, at two we had *tiffin* (lunch) – and we wanted it.

By four o'clock the work was done and I went home. Around six, I went for a drive with my wife. Our drive usually ended at the club, where we met nearly everyone in the station, both men and women. About 7.30 we drove home to dinner, and were generally in bed and asleep soon after nine.

(From: John Beames, *The Memoirs of a Bengali Civilian*. London: Chatto & Windus, 1964)

2
The Attitude of the British Administrators

'It was service, service, service every time.' The word runs like a response through the litanies of 'Anglo-India'. Even those outside the military or the civil administration used it when referring to the 'tour of service' by which they were contracted to their employers. It was part of an often unconscious attitude inherited [...] by all those who made their careers in India: 'We realized that we were members of a very successful race. We belonged to a country that had done exceedingly well for a small island. And we also realized that we were working in a country which was as pre-eminently unsuccessful as we were successful. And I suppose that produced a frame of mind in which we *tacitly* – not explicitly – felt ourselves to be rather superior people.' The superiority was stressed by authority at an early age, whether in the office, the tea garden or the court of law, and it was accepted without question. As assistant Superintendent of Police at nineteen, Geoge Carroll had authority over hundreds of policemen in the district: 'The question of exercising my power never arose in my mind because it seemed so natural that, as an Englishman, I should have power over all my Indian subordinates!'

(From: Charles Allen, ed., *Plain Tales from the Raj. Images of British India in the Twentieth Century*. Newton Abbot: Readers Union, 1976)

4 **be contracted to sb.**: have a contract with sb. 10 **tacit** ['tæsɪt]: stillschweigend
17 **subordinate**: Untergebener

3
British Women in India

The British women in India [...] could be divided into three groups:

1. A few who loathed everything about India and only wanted to leave for good as soon as possible. They could go home while their husbands stayed on in India. This almost inevitably led to the break-up of their marriages. Or the wife could sacrifice herself out of love and loyalty for her husband and stay with him. This was also likely to lead to ther break-up of their marriage because of the great strain imposed on both of them. Or, her husband might resign from service in India, take his wife home and find another job. The key to the survival of the marriage would probably be his getting at least as good a job in the United Kingdom as he had held in India. This last solution was hardly ever resorted to.
2. A much larger number of women loved the life in India. These were found most frequently amongst those who took full advantage of the sports that India had to offer – tennis, riding, hunting, shooting, fishing, camping, trekking [...], and perhaps one should add dancing and entertaining. Most of these women were young. As they grew older, most of them would join the third group described below.
3. (Most women belonged to) those who in the North enjoyed the cold weather but dreaded the hot weather and rains in the plains, and those in the South who disliked the hot moist weather lasting through most of the year, but who steeled themselves in either case to endure with the help of one or two short visits to the hills. These were the hardier souls. But in the North it was not at all unusual for wives with the approval of their husbands to stay up in the hills for the full five months from May to September. If there were small children it was essential to keep them in the hills for the full five months. Some of the women found they had reserves within themselves which made it easier to put with the climate, the stupidity of the servants,

2 **loathe sb./sth.**: hate sb./sth. 5 **sacrifice yourself**: sich opfern 12 **resort to sth.**: make use of sth. as a means of achieving sth. 24 **hardy**: strong and able to survive

and the confidences with younger women, which they did not want to hear. Such women were indeed lucky and so were their husbands.

[...] The greatest enemy of women in India was boredom. It drove them to drink, to flirt, to hypochondria, to quarrel.

(From: R.V. Vernede, *British Life in India*. Delhi: Oxford University Press, 1995)

4
A British Life Abroad

[British women] never entirely integrated with India and this was terribly important as far as the whole ethos of the Raj was concerned. The men were very closely integrated but not their wives. We were in India, we were looked after by Indian servants and we met a great many Indians, and some of us undoubtedly made a very close study of India and Indian customs, but once you stepped inside the home you were back in Cheltenham or Bath. We brought with us in our home lives almost exact replicas of the sort of life that upper middle class people lived in England at that time. It was very homogenous in the sense that nearly everyone in official India sprang from precisely the same educational and cultural background. You went from bungalow to bungalow and you found the same sort of furniture, the same sort of dinner table set, the same kind of conversation. We read the same books, mostly imported by post from England, and I can't really say that we took an awful lot from India.

(From: Vere Birdwood, in: Charles Allen, ed, *Plain Tales from the Raj*, Newton Abbot: Readers Union, 1976)

8 **replica**: good or exact copy of sth.

The Author

© Bernard Gotfryd/Getty Images, Hulton Archive

Ruth Prawer Jhabvala was born in Cologne in 1927 into a comfortable, middle-class Jewish family. In 1939 they left Nazi Germany and emigrated to Britain, where Jhabvala attended school. She graduated from London University with an MA in English literature. At the age of 24 she married Cyrus Jhabvala, an Indian Parsi architect, and moved to New Delhi. The couple have three daughters.

In India Prawer Jhabvala started writing novels and short stories about her new surroundings, portraying various aspects of Indian middle-class life and manners. She also examined the interaction between Westerners and Western life and Indians and Indian culture. Her best-known novel remains *Heat and Dust* (1975), for which she received the Booker Prize; it was filmed in 1983, with Prawer Jhabvala herself writing the script of the filmed version.

In 1975 she and her husband settled in New York and she eventually became a US citizen. This move was accompanied by a literary shift away from India as the subject and the location of her fiction. In the narrative *In Search of Love and Beauty* (1983) she turned to her German-Jewish background and immigrants in New York.

But apart from *Heat and Dust*, she is best known for her work as scriptwriter for Merchant Ivory Productions, for which she has written more than 20 screenplays, including *Shakespeare Wallah* (1965) and the adapted screenplays of Forster's novels *A Room with a View* (1985) and *Howards End* (1992), for which she received Academy Awards.

For most of her life Jhabvala has remained an outsider wherever she has lived and this feeling of otherness has had a considerable influence on her work.